To Ellie Pankin
with all best wishes —
Marjorie Blanchard

Elle Pankin

T2-FHQ-364

THE VEGETARIAN MENU COOKBOOK

THE VEGETARIAN MENU COOKBOOK

by Marjorie Page Blanchard

in consultation with Katy Bucher

illustrated by Ellen Wong

A COOKING PLUS BOOK

Franklin Watts
New York | London | 1979

Library of Congress Cataloging in Publication Data

Blanchard, Marjorie P
    The vegetarian menu cookbook.

    (A Cooking plus book)
    Bibliography: p.
    Includes index.
    SUMMARY: A guide to preparing vegetarian
dishes for a variety of occasions. Includes the
calorie count and nutritional value of each dish.
    1. Vegetarian cookery—Juvenile literature. [1.
Vegetarian cookery 2. Cookery] I. Wong, Ellen.
II. Title.
TX837.B55   641.5′636   78–12959
ISBN 0–531–01497–5

Text copyright © 1979 by Marjorie Page Blanchard
Illustrations copyright © 1979 by Franklin Watts, Inc.
All rights reserved
Printed in the United States of America
5   4   3   2   1

CONTENTS

FOREWORD

This book provides recipes, nutrition notes, and menu suggestions that can guide the young person in the planning and preparation of a nutritionally sound vegetarian diet.

Many times when young people turn to a vegetarian diet, they continue their eating habits as usual, except for the exclusion of meats, fish, and poultry. As a result, their diets tend to be nutritionally haphazard, monotonous, and their new style of eating is short-lived. However, with proper planning, vegetarian diets can be nutritionally sound, varied, and a perfectly healthy way to eat.

Katy Bucher
Dietician and Nutritionist
Bridgeport Hospital
Bridgeport, Conn.

(Protein and caloric values for recipes and menus were calculated from nutrient data in U.S.D.A. *Handbook #456, Food Uses of Portions Commonly Used* by Bowes and Church, and from manufacturers' data.)

THE VEGETARIAN MENU COOKBOOK

INTRODUCTION

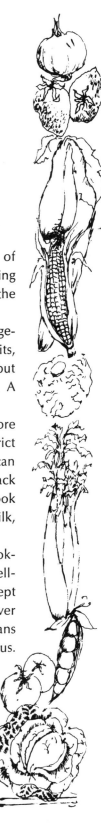

This book is about a new kind of eating based on a lot of old familiar foods. Every book should have a reason for being printed in the first place and usually that reason answers the questions, What? Why? When? Who? Where?

What is a vegetarian? According to the dictionary a vegetarian is a person who lives solely on vegetables, grains, fruits, and nuts. Actually the word is not derived from "vegetable" but from the Latin *vegetus* meaning whole, sound, fresh, lively. A nice way to be in any language.

Nutritionists have found, however, that we do need more protein for a balanced diet than we would get from being strict vegetarians or Vegans as they are called. Too strict a diet can be dangerous as it can lead to a calcium deficiency and a lack of vitamin B_{12}. Therefore, for the purposes of health, this book is based on a lacto-ovo-vegetarian diet that includes eggs, milk, and milk products such as cheese.

Why is a vegetarian cookbook important? Vegetarian cooking is based on just one idea: Meat is not necessary to a well-rounded diet. And these days this is an important concept because of the high cost of meat and a shortage of food all over the world. We have all been told many times that Americans eat too much meat—and that it isn't necessarily good for us.

We know that there are millions of starving people in the world and we were all told as children to "eat up because someone else is going hungry."

When we are older, we realize that the solution to this hunger is obviously not to send our leftovers to other countries. It is simply to eat less wastefully and make what we eat count. By eliminating animal protein from our diet and concentrating on the proper combinations of other foods we can achieve this goal. We will not only be healthier but also happier in the knowledge that we are helping to conserve the world's food supply.

If you decide that you would like to try the vegetarian style of eating just to see what it's all about, it is only right to give the diet a fair test. This cookbook is designed to make your test run as a vegetarian go smoothly. It must not be a hit-or-miss series of meals based on bananas and nuts with some raw carrots and cooked soybeans on the side. If you are going to try something as important as a new diet—and anything to do with your health and body is important—you should approach it sensibly, not just on the well-meaning advice of a friend who "tried it once." (Maybe your friend was just born healthy with a good figure and lots of energy.)

Make this a well-planned experiment, as you would with any new venture you are undertaking. Read up on it. We'll give you the basics as to what your body needs and how to supply these needs. We'll show you how to plan and cook meals that look good, taste good, and satisfy all your nutritional needs without meat, chicken, or fish.

When should you eat an all vegetable diet? If the vegetables are supplemented with dairy products and eggs, these meals can be eaten every day.

To understand why this is so, you need some basic information about protein. Protein is essential to life and growth, especially for teen-agers. The average teen-ager needs at least 48 grams a day. Protein is made up of amino acids. There are 22 amino acids in all. The most complete source of protein and the essential amino acids are the animal and dairy sources—

meat, fish, poultry, milk, eggs, and cheese. The other, but in-
complete, source of protein is plant material such as dried
legumes, nuts, and grains. The healthy person can synthesize 14
of the 22 amino acids within his or her own body. The other
8 must be obtained from food and, for perfect body-building,
they must be eaten together at the same meal. The question is,
how do you do this without meat protein? The answer is, by
making winning combinations of foods that together supply all
of the essential amino acids. Because dairy products are complete
in themselves, they become the easy-to-add foods that are
essential to any nutritionally sound vegetarian diet. That extra
glass of milk is very important with the meal or snack.

Do you see now why a cookbook for this kind of eating would come in handy? Once you get into the swing of it you will begin to plan complete vegetable protein meals automatically. As a matter of fact, some of these combinations may already be part of your daily diet. It's easy to remember the right combinations once you become familiar with them.

Another word about protein. The diet we are recommending could be described as "high protein." That is, it provides almost twice as much protein as the recommended daily allowance. Why don't we cut your protein intake in half? Because, being an American, this is what you are used to. In this country most of us consume more protein than people do elsewhere in the world, and at this important stage of your growth and development, it does not make sense for you to cut back to subsistence level, especially if you are starting on a new pattern of eating.

Who can eat a lacto-ovo-vegetarian meal? Anyone as long as he or she checks with a doctor first. Discuss it with your physician, showing that you know what it is all about from a nutrition angle; that you are not going off on some kind of crazy fad diet; and that you will continue to eat three sensible meals a day, with snacks if necessary.

Incidentally, you are probably thinking at this point, "What makes anyone think I get three complete meals a day anyhow? They should see our school lunches." All the more reason for you to try this kind of eating. It will probably be healthier than what you've been doing up to now—skipping meals and snacking.

Where can you get all these foods? Just look around you. They are everywhere—in the garden, on the pantry shelf, in the dairy case, in the bakery department. All of the ingredients for a good vegetarian diet are easy to find if you know what to look for. And that is what you're going to find out in this book.

GUIDELINES

THE FAMOUS FOUR

Four food groups are essential to the protein part of a meat-less diet. At a meal you should combine foods from two or more of the groups, then supplement with vegetables and fruits to add necessary vitamins and minerals.

Doing this may sound confusing, but it is really much less difficult than that math problem that gave you such fits yesterday and if you've ever worked a computer, this will seem like a breeze.

  I.   Legumes: beans, peanuts, lentils, peas
 II.   Grains: wheat, corn, rice, barley, breads, cereals
III.   Seeds: sunflower, pumpkin, sesame
 IV.   Dairy products: milk, cheese, eggs, yogurt, buttermilk

Sprinkle on for extra protein:

nonfat dry milk
soy flour
wheat germ
grated cheese
any seeds
nuts

The dark, leafy greens such as spinach, lettuce, watercress, and chard are important for vitamins A and C. They also provide calcium, riboflavin, and folacin. And don't underrate the importance of eye appeal. Bright orange carrots with green peas, red, red tomatoes with dark green spinach, golden corn and pale-green limas all look—and taste—delicious.

Fruit is a natural source of vitamins, especially C, which is easily destroyed by the heat in cooking. There's more than pretty poetry in that line about "an apple a day" and what better way to get your daily vitamin C than to eat a bowl of juicy ripe strawberries.

THE CARBOHYDRATE QUESTION

We read a lot about empty calories. What does the phrase really mean? It means simply that certain calorie sources—overprocessed carbohydrates, simple sugars, and some fats—are nutritionally inferior. They give you a quick lift, a fast spurt of energy (Coke and Danish, for instance), but do not provide other vitamins and minerals. If you take a spoonful of honey, it will provide a rapid postprandial rise in blood glucose (quick energy). The body cells will metabolize this glucose for immediate energy or change it into fat for stored energy.

While sugars, honey, molasses, and refined starches add interest and flavor to a diet, they should be limited because they won't add any of the other nutrients we need. Try to think of the value of foods in terms of "nutrient density"—or how many nutrients you get per calorie. In talking about "empty" and "full" calories, we are actually talking about a balance of nutrients. Empty calories, or those that come from foods high in sugar or fat, should be avoided in favor of foods that are rich in vitamins, minerals, or protein. Although empty calories won't add weight unless you exceed in total calorie intake what you expend in energy, it is certainly much better to use your carbo-

hydrate calories on whole grain breads, cereals, and good fruits, which also give you energy but with more staying power.

If you are really worried about gaining weight—you are overweight now or have the tendency to be—then there are certain rules you can follow as you go along with our suggested menus.

1. Skimp on your own portions; use a small plate and spread the food out on it.

2. Make your plate look attractive using sprigs of parsley, carrot curls, and other edible vegetable decorations to fill in empty spaces.

3. Avoid the luxury foods. By this we don't mean those foods that cost a lot; we mean the delicious but disastrous dishes such as fried foods, hot breads with butter, sauces, salad dressings, and rich desserts. Substitute low-fat cheese or skim milk if you are really hungry.

4. Don't skip meals; you will be much hungrier when the next one arrives.

5. Eat slowly.

Be forewarned: The suggested menus are not at all low in calories. Calorie requirements vary widely, so you may want to think twice before digging into all the luscious desserts on the menus. On the other hand, if you don't have a weight problem, let appetite be your guide.

ONCE A DAY

Try to include in your daily diet:

raw fruit or fresh fruit juice
a green salad using the leafy dark greens
whole grain cereal or bread
3 to 4 glasses of milk or the same amount of yogurt
fresh vegetables

JUST FOR FUN . . .

Go through our menus for the week and see how we rate on combining food groups in a meal. You'll find that we have managed to combine more than two groups in each meal—such as chutney beans, spinach salad with sesame seeds and fruit-and-cheese pie, or cheese-stuffed zucchini, brown rice and almonds, and ice-cream sandwiches. To make blue Monday a brighter day, we've started with whole wheat apple-nut-raisin muffins that you can whip up on Sunday—while you get yourself mentally prepared for the vegetarian week ahead.

The total gram protein and calorie count is noted at the top of each menu page. It is figured for the total amount you eat that day, including dishes that are not in the recipe index, such as spinach salad, raw mushrooms, cranberry juice. The count is given for one average serving, no seconds.

A note on metrics: You will notice that metric measures are given in parentheses in every recipe. There is some confusion about how American cooks will use the metric system when it becomes commonplace. Will we, for example, translate 1 cup to 240 milliliters or to .24 liters? Or will we round it out to ¼ liter? Will we measure flour by weight as the Europeans do, or will we continue to measure flour in a cup? I have used milliliters instead of fractions of liters and I have assumed that Americans will continue to measure dry ingredients by volume.

TEST YOURSELF WITH
A WEEK'S WORTH OF VEGETABLES

The best way to try anything really new is to slip into it lightly with a trial run. Here we've planned out a whole week of menus—breakfast, lunch, dinner, and snacks—for you to use. Mix or match them as you like, just so you get your protein allowance and full nutrition for the day. We guarantee that you'll feel fuller with less food and possibly lose a pound or two in the bargain.

Suggestion: Choose a vacation week to try this out. It is very hard to do anything correctly for the first time on the run. This is really creative cooking and it will be fun if you have the time to think about it.

To begin at the beginning:

CALLING UP THE RESERVES

Up to now, breakfast may be the meal you skip because there just isn't time to eat it before school—and it is always a choice of eggs or cereal. Boring.

But, breakfast is your first meal in about 12 hours and if you miss it your body has to summon all of its resources to get through the next 4 or 5 hours until lunch. This means that your body is borrowing from its storage supply of vitamins and calcium to keep going because you haven't supplied it with the nutrients for the day's activities. In short, the engine will be running a bit rough.

A person who skips breakfast tends to be tired, cross, and hard to live with. Your problems with teachers and studies loom large and your friends and their problems become impossible. Everything is more down than up and you just don't have any energy. There is today's key word: *energy*. Our sources of energy have become very important to us and our own body is one of the most important sources we have—that we can completely control. It's amazing what you can accomplish when you feel alive and electric—and what happens when you run out of power.

So start with breakfast, which by all rights should provide between one quarter and one third of the day's total food requirements: vitamins, minerals, protein, and calories. And if you plan breakfast for the family, you can be sure of having a meal that you'll enjoy, plus having someone to eat it with. Who could resist sliced oranges sprinkled with cinnamon, or corn fritters and apple rings, or cottage cheese pancakes, or special French toast? It's worth getting up for.

Nutrition Note: We are suggesting milk to accompany most of the meals to provide protein, calcium, B_{12}, and riboflavin.

THE LARGER LUNCH

Actually, lunch should be a bigger meal than dinner because you've still got a lot of the day left to go and you need a lot of energy. If you're eating in the school cafeteria it's not too easy to have exactly what we suggest here, but you may be able to work around the school lunch or possibly bring your own. If there are enough of your friends interested in good healthy food, you might get a committee together and go to the principal to suggest changes in the lunch menu. Put your ideas on the basis of health and cost and make the principal realize that less food would be wasted if you were offered more of the foods that students would eat, instead of what we call junk foods. Then lunch could be a good meal instead of one you skip or waste.

Remember: Skipping lunch always leads to snacks, which in turn leads to extra calories, which in turn leads to not looking so slim in last summer's bathing suit.

SIT DOWN AND RELAX

Dinner—which comes between homework and telephone calls—is the time to take a breathing spell. Even if you don't have much time it can still be a good, and exciting, meal. This is the meal that will be altered the most by a vegetarian regime be-

cause usually dinner is planned with meat as the central theme. A starch, a vegetable or a salad, and dessert are tacked on and that's it night after night. By leaving out the meat you can make the main course something inventive like chutney beans, a cheese fondue with apples, or stuffed zucchini. Start with a hot tomato or cold blueberry soup and follow up with baked pears or a cool lemon freeze. You'll have a dinner that's worth sitting down for, and eating it will be half the fun.

THE FAST FOOD FAD

Nobody can deny that fast foods are part of our lives today simply because we're always on the move. Fast foods are quick and easy—and they're also many times called junk food.

There is a difference between fast and junk. While riding your bicycle you can chew on a snack that is a fast food but doesn't have to qualify as junk. Just for starters, what about granola bars, homemade corn chips, peanut butter popcorn, or yogurt pops? Try oatmeal chews, sesame sticks, or nut brittle—or a super strawberry shake. These will all take the edge off your appetite while giving you something nourishing to chew on. And they're great party foods. Also less expensive than all of the commercially packed snacks. Unless your allowance is princely, that can make a big difference.

MENUS AND RECIPES FOR A WEEK

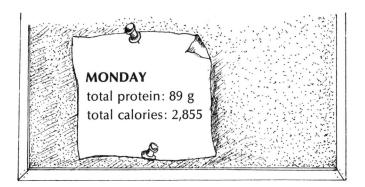

MONDAY
total protein: 89 g
total calories: 2,855

BREAKFAST
oatmeal with cinnamon and raisins
sliced peaches with fruit yogurt
whole grain toast
milk

LUNCH
grilled peanut butter and tomato on granola bread
maple custard
milk

DINNER
macaroni and three cheeses
tossed green salad
baked pears with streusel topping
milk

Snack: 6 mushroom caps stuffed with
1½ oz. (43 g) cream cheese
and chives, a glass of milk

Are sugars really the villain in the kitchen? If you cut out all sugars would you lose weight automatically? In the first place, it would be almost impossible to do that because one quarter of all sugars consumed come from fruit and dairy products. These are called "fructose" and "lactose." In the second place, there is no evidence to prove that carbohydrate calories (including sugar) have any more to do with weight gain than any other calories. Each person has to have a balance between energy output and energy input to keep a steady weight and as far as energy is concerned sugar calories are no different from the rest of the calories your body takes in. The big difference comes in what *type* of sugar foods you eat because some, such as candy, contain few other nutrients in relation to their caloric value. Here again is the nutrient density concept as mentioned on page 8.

So, don't shy away from a *nutritious* sweet dessert (which can do wonders for your morale) just thinking about your new bathing suit. Choose a dessert with a fruit or dairy product base and cut down on the size of the portion, if you're worried.

We have not allowed for seconds in the daily count, but each person is different in his or her need for food; if you want more to fill you up, then eat more. If you are gaining weight, cut back.

MAPLE CUSTARD

protein: 6 g   calories: 155

    3 eggs
    2 cups (480 ml) milk
    ½ cup (120 ml) maple syrup
    ¼ tsp (1.25 ml) salt

1. Break eggs into bowl and beat until foamy.
2. Pour milk into saucepan. Add maple syrup and heat just until

bubbles begin to show at the edge of the pan and there is steam rising from the milk. Stir occasionally so as not to burn the milk on the bottom of the pan.

3. Pour the hot milk into the bowl with the eggs, beating the entire time.

4. Using a measuring cup or a ladle, pour the custard into six custard cups.

5. Set the cups in a pan of hot water.

6. Set the pan in a preheated 325°F (160°C) oven on the middle shelf and bake for 40 minutes until the custard looks firm.

7. Take the cups out of the pan and let them cool.

8. Refrigerate when cool.

Yield: 6 servings

Note: If you do happen to burn some milk on the bottom of the saucepan, fill it halfway with water and add 1 tbsp (15 ml) baking soda. Put the pan on high heat and boil the water until you can scrape off the burned milk with a spoon.

MACARONI AND THREE CHEESES

protein: 18 g   calories: 495

8 oz. (226.8 g) macaroni
4 tbsp (60 ml) butter
4 tbsp (60 ml) all-purpose white flour
2 cups (480 ml) milk
1 tbsp (15 ml) minced onion
¼ cup (60 ml) each shredded Mozzarella, grated Parmesan,
    shredded Cheddar

1.   Cook macaroni according to directions on package.
2.   Meanwhile, heat butter in saucepan and add onion. Cook
for 3 minutes. Add flour and cook for 2 minutes, stirring. Add
milk and cook, stirring, until thick and smooth. Add cheeses and
blend.
3.   Mix sauce with macaroni and turn into buttered casserole.
4.   Bake for 30 minutes in 350°F (175°C) oven until bubbling.

Yield: 4 servings

BAKED PEARS
WITH STREUSEL TOPPING

protein: 4 g   calories: 460

4 ripe pears or 8 canned pear halves
Juice of 1 lemon
½ cup (120 ml) butter or margarine
½ cup (120 ml) brown sugar
¼ cup (60 ml) all-purpose white flour
¼ cup (60 ml) toasted wheat germ
¼ tsp (1.2 ml) ground ginger

1.   Peel pears, core and cut in halves. Place in one layer in buttered 1-quart baking dish. Sprinkle with lemon juice. If using canned pears, drain and place in baking dish.

2.   Put butter, sugar, flour, wheat germ, and ginger into large bowl. With mixer or fingertips, blend mixture thoroughly until it resembles coarse crumbs. Spread over pears.

3.   Bake for 30 minutes in 350°F (175°C) oven.
    Serve warm.

Yield: 4 servings

JANUARY

Monday I

_____

TUESDAY
total protein: 105 g
total calories: 2,795

_____

Wednesday 3

BREAKFAST
sliced cheese grilled on whole wheat toast with avocado
sliced oranges sprinkled with cinnamon
milk

LUNCH
corn, rice, and green bean salad
crunchy crackers
fresh strawberries
milk

DINNER
stuffed zucchini with tomato sauce
brown rice and almonds
super ice-cream sandwiches
milk

Snack: ½ cup (120 ml) lentil sprouts mixed with ¼ cup (60 ml)
sesame seeds on ½ cup (120 ml) cottage cheese

There have been a lot of changes in eating habits since most of you were born, and you are lucky enough to be living at a very interesting and exciting time in the history of food. About ten years ago, a prophecy was made that by now cooking would be almost nonexistent. Almost all food would be frozen and people could simply dial instructions to their freezer from wherever they happened to be and by the time they got home the food would be hot and ready to eat.

That sounds like the easy way out of food marketing and preparation, a sort of outer-space idea, but luckily it hasn't happened and probably won't. We do have many more convenience foods today, but more and more people, including you, are right in the kitchen fixing the foods you are going to eat—and knowing exactly what goes in them. Making your own crackers might sound a bit silly, for instance, when there are so many kinds on the market, but we guarantee you'll find these homemade ones tastier—you can flavor them any way you like—and a lot of fun.

Food is so much a part of everyone's life and here you're in on the ground floor because what you eat is up to you—including ice-cream sandwiches.

CORN, RICE, AND
GREEN BEAN SALAD

protein: 4 g   calories: 185

    1 cup (240 ml) corn kernels, fresh or frozen
    1 cup (240 ml) cooked rice
    1 cup (240 ml) green beans
    1 tbsp (15 ml) chopped green pepper
    3 tbsp (45 ml) vinaigrette dressing

1.   Cook corn kernels in a little boiling, salted water for 2 minutes. Drain well.
2.   Cut green beans into ½-inch (1.25-cm) lengths and cook in boiling, salted water for 5 minutes. Drain and run under cold water. Dry on paper towels.
3.   Put corn, rice, beans, and green pepper into a bowl.
4.   Sprinkle with salad dressing and toss altogether. Chill.

Yield: 3 servings

FRENCH VINAIGRETTE DRESSING

protein: 0 g   calories: 65 per tbsp

    ⅓ cup (80 ml) vinegar
    1 tsp (5 ml) sugar
    1 tsp (5 ml) prepared mustard
    1 tsp (5 ml) salt
    Freshly ground pepper
    ⅔ cup (160 ml) oil

Mix in order given. Stir or shake well. Store in refrigerator.

Yield: 1 cup (240 ml)

CRUNCHY CRACKERS

protein: 4 g   calories: 160 (6 crackers)

    2 cups (480 ml) unbleached white flour
    1 tsp (5 ml) salt
    ½ tsp (2.5 ml) baking soda
    2 tbsp (30 ml) shortening
    ⅔ cup (160 ml) buttermilk

1. In a large bowl combine flour, salt, and soda.

2. With fingertips or pastry blender work in the shortening until the mixture resembles coarse meal.

3. Stir in the buttermilk and mix until you have a soft dough.

4. Turn the dough out onto a floured counter and beat on it for a few minutes with your fists.

5. To make dough easier to work with, divide it into several pieces. Lightly grease a flat cookie sheet (one without sides). Put the dough on the cookie sheet, and with a floured rolling pin, roll it out very thin. Do this with as many pieces as will fit onto the sheet.

6. Using a sharp knife, pizza cutter, or pie wheel, cut the dough into squares or diamonds.

7. Preheat the oven to 375°F (190°C). Bake for 15 minutes until lightly browned. The length of baking time depends on how thin the dough is.

8. Take the crackers off the sheet with a spatula and put them on racks to cool. Store in a covered container.

Yield: 3 dozen crackers

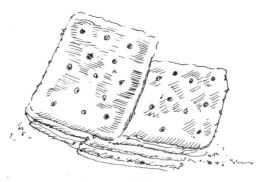

STUFFED ZUCCHINI

protein: 15 g   calories: 250

1 1-lb. (.45 kg) zucchini
1 carrot
1 stalk celery
½ small onion
1 clove garlic
½ cup (120 ml) ricotta or cottage cheese
1 egg
2 tbsp (30 ml) parsley
Salt to taste
Freshly ground pepper
2 tbsp (30 ml) grated Parmesan cheese

1. Cut zucchini in half the long way and scoop out the center.
2. Mix together the scooped-out zucchini, carrot, celery, and onion. Chop fine. Mince the garlic. Mix chopped vegetables with garlic and ricotta or cottage cheese. Stir in the egg and parsley. Season with salt and pepper.
3. Fill zucchini halves with this mixture.
4. Sprinkle grated cheese over the top and bake for 20 minutes in a preheated 350°F (175°C) oven.

Yield: 2 servings

BROWN RICE AND ALMONDS

protein: 10 g   calories: 580

¼ lb. (113.40 g) butter or margarine
1 cup (240 ml) brown rice
1 cup (240 ml) blanched toasted almonds
3 cups (720 ml) vegetable broth
Salt to taste
Freshly ground pepper

1.   Melt butter in heavy skillet and add rice. Stir rice until lightly browned.
2.   Add almonds and turn into greased 1½-quart (1.7 l) casserole.
3.   Pour in vegetable broth and season.
4.   Cover and place in preheated 350°F (175°C) oven. Bake for 30 minutes.
5.   Uncover and bake for 30 to 45 minutes longer, until rice has absorbed liquid.

Yield: 4 servings

SUPER ICE-CREAM SANDWICHES

protein: 6 g   calories: 305

½ cup (120 ml) butter or margarine
1 cup (240 ml) molasses
1 cup (240 ml) sugar
2 eggs, beaten
4 cups (960 ml) all-purpose white flour
1 tsp (5 ml) salt
1 tsp (5 ml) baking soda
1 tsp (5 ml) ginger
2 tsp (10 ml) cinnamon
¾ cup (180 ml) milk
Vanilla ice-cream

1.   Melt butter in large saucepan. Stir in molasses and mix over low heat until well blended.
2.   Remove from heat and stir in sugar and beaten eggs.
3.   Mix together in a bowl the flour, salt, baking soda, ginger, and cinnamon.
4.   Add the dry ingredients to the molasses mixture alternately with the milk. Beat well with a wooden spoon or mixer after each addition. Beat the whole mixture until smooth.
5.   Drop rounded measuring tablespoons of the mixture onto greased baking sheets. Allow room between each one as they will spread to about 4 inches (10 cm) in diameter.
6.   Bake in a 350°F (175°C) oven for 12 to 14 minutes. Remove to racks with spatula.
7.   Put two cookies together with vanilla ice-cream slices.
8.   Wrap in foil and place in freezer.

Yield: one dozen

WEDNESDAY
total protein: 81 g
total calories: 2,665

BREAKFAST
musli
whole wheat apple-nut-raisin muffins with butter
milk

LUNCH
curried egg and avocado in a pita pocket
cranberry juice on ice
milk

DINNER
chutney beans
spinach salad with raw mushrooms and sesame-seed dressing
fruit-and-cheese pie in whole wheat crust
milk

Snack: 2 slices rye bread with ¼ cup ricotta cheese,
        sprinkled with 1 tbsp (15 ml) chopped nuts,
        small glass orange juice

Musli is a crunchy, nutritious breakfast dish that we borrow from the Swiss. Undoubtedly Heidi thrived on musli, which combines oatmeal with fruit juice, apples, honey, and nuts.

Though we hear about eating a "good breakfast," there is still a tendency in the American diet to skimp on, or skip, the first meal of the day. There are many reasons for this, probably the main one being lack of time. Of course, we could use that as an excuse for never eating a meal at all but it is true that many people do not feel particularly hungry immediately after getting out of bed. At first, you may have to use a lot of willpower to make yourself cook a breakfast.

Look upon breakfast as part of a good change in your eating habits, and for heaven's sake, make it interesting! If you head for the cold cereal box every single morning, no wonder you think about skipping the whole thing. Start considering the possibilities of exciting breakfasts. There is no reason why you can't have fruit and cottage cheese, grilled cheese sandwiches, soups, or corn fritters first thing in the morning, and it may smell so good cooking that you'll attract a few more members of the family to the breakfast table. We'll bet that your father will be right there!

MUSLI

---

protein: 9 g   calories: 370

3 tbsp (45 ml) oatmeal
9 tbsp (135 ml) cold milk, water, or orange juice
1 tbsp (15 ml) lemon juice
1 tbsp (15 ml) heavy cream
1 apple, grated
1 tbsp (15 ml) chopped nuts
Honey or brown sugar to taste
Seasonal fruits (optional)

1.   Soak oatmeal overnight in milk, water, or orange juice. Refrigerate.
2.   In the morning add the lemon juice, cream, apple, nuts, and sweeten to taste.
3.   If there is fresh fruit in season, add it to the mixture. You may also stir in yogurt if you wish.

Yield: 1 serving

WHOLE WHEAT
APPLE-NUT-RAISIN MUFFINS

protein: 3 g   calories: 135

 1 egg
 ½ cup (120 ml) milk
 ¼ cup (60 ml) melted butter or margarine
 1½ cups (360 ml) whole wheat flour
 2 tsp (10 ml) baking powder
 ½ tsp (2.5 ml) salt
 ½ cup (120 ml) sugar
 1 tsp (5 ml) cinnamon
 ½ tsp (2.5 ml) nutmeg
 1 cup (240 ml) unpeeled coarsely chopped apple

1.   In large bowl beat together the egg, milk, and butter.
2.   Combine flour, baking powder, salt, sugar, cinnamon, and nutmeg. Stir into egg mixture. Mix in apple and blend well.
3.   Fill greased muffin tins two-thirds full.
4.   Bake in a preheated 400°F (200°C) oven for 20 minutes.

Yield: 12 muffins

CURRIED EGG AND AVOCADO IN A PITA POCKET

protein: 12 g   calories: 465

1 hard-boiled egg
Mayonnaise
Salt to taste
Freshly ground pepper
Curry powder to taste
½ avocado, peeled and sliced
Watercress, stems and leaves
1 whole wheat pita or Syrian bread

1.   In a small bowl mash the egg with the mayonnaise. Season to your own liking with salt, pepper, and curry powder. Go lightly on the curry, starting with a pinch.
2.   Split the pita and spread with the egg mixture.
3.   Top with avocado slices and put watercress on top.

Yield: 1 serving

CHUTNEY BEANS

protein: 10 g   calories: 250

 ¼ cup (60 ml) mango chutney, minced
 1 tsp (5 ml) prepared mustard
 1 tbsp (15 ml) minced onion
 2 tbsp (30 ml) molasses
 1 1-lb. (.45 kg) can baked beans
 2 tomatoes, sliced

1. In large bowl mix chutney, mustard, onion, and molasses.
2. Add beans and mix all together gently.
3. Turn into a 1-quart baking dish and top with sliced tomatoes.
4. Bake 30 minutes in a 350°F (175°C) oven until bubbling.

Yield: 3 servings

SESAME SEED DRESSING

protein: 0 g   calories: 60 per tbsp

 1 tbsp (15 ml) vinegar
 ¼ tsp (1.25 ml) salt
 Freshly ground pepper
 3 tbsp (45 ml) oil
 1 tsp (5 ml) sesame seeds
 1 tsp (5 ml) chopped parsley

Mix ingredients in order given, blending well.

Yield: ⅓ cup (80 ml)

THURSDAY
total protein: 80 g
total calories: 2,375

BREAKFAST
lacy corn fritters
glazed apple rings
broiled tomatoes
milk

LUNCH
Greek salad
corn chips
golden pineapple rings
milk

DINNER
omelets with mushrooms and cream cheese
oven potato sticks
cucumber and green pepper strips with yogurt-lemon dressing
spicy apple flan
milk

Snack: 1 slice Boston brown bread (canned) with 1 oz. (28.6 g)
cream cheese mixed with 1 tsp (5 ml) chopped dates,
milk

Protein is an overworked word. We've all read about hi-pro
everything from bread to diet and we are generally inclined to
think that protein must come largely from animal sources. You
are finding out, by eating a lot of different foods (no more
hamburger and fried chicken), that this is not necessarily so. You
are also realizing the importance of having a diet balanced in
protein, fat, and carbohydrate. In this way, your fat and carbo-

hydrate intake provide sufficient calories in the overall diet to let the protein do its major job of growth and tissue repair.

On this same subject of protein, you may have heard the expression "eating lower on the food chain." That is exactly what you will be doing on this diet by eating protein from plant rather than animal sources. You are, in effect, cutting out the "middle-man" as you derive the protein directly from its prime source without having it go into the cow, then into you. It's nice to know that as you help your own health you are also helping that of someone else in this small, small world.

LACY CORN FRITTERS

protein: 3 g   calories: 120

    1 cup (240 ml) corn kernels, fresh or frozen
    1 egg
    1 tsp (5 ml) sugar
    ½ tsp (2.5 ml) baking powder
    ½ tsp (2.5 ml) salt
    2 to 3 tbsp (30 to 45 ml) all-purpose white flour
    Shortening

1.   Cook corn in a little water for 2 minutes. Drain and put into a small bowl.
2.   Mix in the egg, sugar, baking powder, salt, and enough flour to make a batter that will hold together when dropped from a spoon. It should not be too runny.
3.   Heat shortening in a skillet until bubbling.
4.   Drop the fritter mixture into the fat by spoonfuls. Fry like pancakes. When brown on one side, turn and brown on the other side.

Serve with maple syrup.

Yield: 4 servings

GLAZED APPLE RINGS

protein: 0   calories: 170

3 tart apples
1 tbsp (15 ml) cinnamon and 3 tbsp (45 ml) sugar, mixed
¼ cup (60 ml) butter

1. Peel and core apples and slice into rings ½ inch (1.25 cm) thick.
2. Put sugar-cinnamon mixture into bowl and dip apple slices in mixture, covering both sides.
3. Heat butter in skillet to bubbling.
4. Put apple rings into butter and brown lightly on both sides.
5. Cover skillet, turn heat to medium, and cook about 7 minutes until apples are tender but not mushy.
6. Remove cover, raise heat, and cook until shiny and glazed.

Yield: 4 servings

GREEK SALAD

protein: 7 g   calories: 200

¼ cup (60 ml) olive oil
Juice of 1 lemon
½ tsp (2.5 ml) salt
Freshly ground pepper
1 10-oz. (283.5 g) package baby lima beans, cooked
1 cucumber, peeled and diced
3 scallions, chopped
2 ripe tomatoes, peeled
2 hard-boiled eggs, quartered
6 black olives
¼ cup (60 ml) feta cheese

1.   In large bowl put oil, lemon juice, salt, and pepper. Mix together with a fork, blending well.
2.   Add lima beans, cucumber, scallions, and tomatoes cut into small pieces. Toss all together.
3.   Sprinkle with crumbled feta cheese and garnish with hard-boiled eggs and olives.

Yield: 6 servings

CORN CHIPS

protein: 1 g   calories: 120 (1/6 of recipe)

½ cup (120 ml) water
3 tbsp (45 ml) melted butter or margarine
2 to 3 drops Tabasco sauce
1 cup (240 ml) yellow cornmeal
½ cup (120 ml) all-purpose white flour
¾ tsp (3.75 ml) salt
¼ tsp (1.25 ml) baking soda

1. Combine water, butter, and Tabasco.
2. In large mixing bowl stir together the cornmeal, flour, salt, and baking soda. Add water mixture and stir until dough forms a ball.
3. Turn out onto floured board and knead for 5 minutes. Divide the dough in half.
4. Grease a large baking sheet with no sides. Place the balls of dough on the sheet and roll out into two 12-inch (30-cm) squares. If they don't come out exactly square, don't worry. You can trim off the edges. Sprinkle with more salt. With a sharp knife or pastry cutter, cut into small squares or triangles.
5. Bake for 12 to 15 minutes in a preheated 350°F (175°C) oven until golden and crisp.
6. Cool and store in covered container.

Yield: 6 servings

GOLDEN PINEAPPLE RINGS

protein: 0   ·calories: 95 (1 ring)

Do you know how to test the ripeness of a fresh pineapple? First, it should have a definite pineapple smell. Second, pull on one of the leaves. If it comes free easily, the fruit is ripe.

1 fresh pineapple or 1 can pineapple slices
⅓ stick butter, melted
Maple syrup

1. Cut off the top and bottom of the pineapple and with a sharp knife, slice it into rings. Then with the point of the knife, cut away the skin and cut out the core.
2. Sprinkle each slice with melted butter and a teaspoonful of maple syrup. Put them on a baking sheet and put under the broiler.
3. Watch carefully and when the syrup is bubbling and shiny, they are ready.

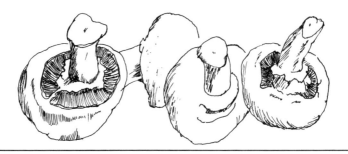

OMELETS WITH MUSHROOMS AND CREAM CHEESE

protein: 13 g   calories: 295

This recipe takes longer to read than it does to do.

4 eggs
4 tsp (20 ml) butter
1½ oz. (42.52 g) cream cheese
4 mushrooms chopped

1.   In a small saucepan heat 2 tsp butter and add cream cheese and mushrooms. Cook until cheese has melted and is mixed into mushrooms.
2.   Make the omelets one at a time. Beat two eggs in bowl.
3.   Heat 1 tsp butter in small frying pan or omelet pan. When butter is sizzling, add eggs.
4.   With fork in one hand and handle of frying pan in the other hand, shake and stir for about 1 minute as if you were making scrambled eggs.
5.   Let eggs cook and as they get done around the edges, swivel the pan around so the wet middle part runs over the edge.
6.   When almost all of the egg is cooked, spoon half the mush-room mixture onto the middle of the omelet. With the fork, lift up one half of the omelet and fold it over the other half. Slide it out of the pan onto a plate. Season with salt and pepper.
7.   Repeat for the second omelet.

Yield: 2 servings

OVEN POTATO STICKS

protein: 5 g   calories: 230

    4 large potatoes
    2 tbsp (30 ml) oil
    Salt

1. Peel potatoes and cut in French-fry sticks.
2. Put oil in large bowl and, with your hands, stir potato sticks so they are coated with oil. Spread out on a baking sheet.
3. Bake for 20 to 30 minutes in a preheated 450°F (230°C) oven until crisp and browned. Stir and turn frequently.
4. Sprinkle with salt while hot.

Yield: 4 servings

YOGURT LEMON DRESSING

protein: 1 g   calories: 40

    ½ cup (120 ml) plain yogurt
    Grated rind of ½ small lemon
    2 tbsp (30 ml) lemon juice
    ½ tsp (2.5 ml) salt
    Freshly ground pepper
    1 tsp (5 ml) chopped mint

Put all ingredients in bowl and mix together with fork. Pour over green pepper and cucumber strips 30 minutes before serving.

Yield: 4 servings

SPICY APPLE FLAN

protein: 9 g   calories: 240

A flan is a custard by any other name, just so you'll know it the next time you see it on a menu.

2 golden Delicious apples
1 tbsp (15 ml) butter
1 tbsp (15 ml) sugar mixed with ½ tsp (2.5 ml) cinnamon
6 eggs
½ cup (120 ml) sugar
2 cups (480 ml) milk
1 tsp (5 ml) vanilla
1 tsp (5 ml) ground nutmeg

1.   Peel and core apples and cut into quarters, then eighths.
2.   Heat butter in large skillet and put in apples, turning to coat all over with melted butter. Sprinkle with cinnamon-sugar mixture and cover pan. Cook over medium heat until apples are tender—about 10 minutes.
3.   With spatula remove apples to 9-inch (22.5-cm) pie pan, arranging to cover bottom of pan completely.
4.   In large bowl beat together the eggs, sugar, milk, and vanilla.
5.   Set pie pan with apples in a larger pan of warm water and place both on baking sheet.
6.   Pour egg mixture over apples. Sprinkle nutmeg over top.
7.   Set baking sheet in oven carefully. Bake for 35 to 45 minutes in a preheated 325°F (160°C) oven until custard is set.
8.   Cool, then refrigerate.

Yield: 6 servings

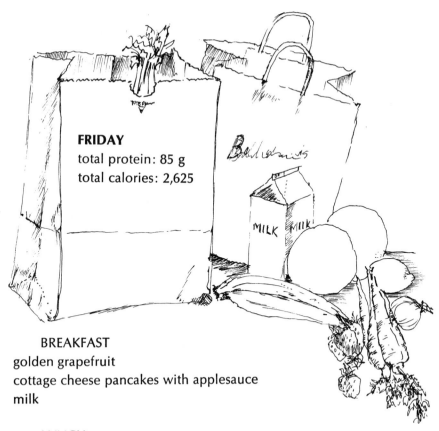

FRIDAY
total protein: 85 g
total calories: 2,625

BREAKFAST
golden grapefruit
cottage cheese pancakes with applesauce
milk

LUNCH
carrots, cream cheese, and raisins on dark bread
strawberry cooler

DINNER
noodle mushroom casserole
Waldorf salad
lemon freeze
milk

Snack: 2 lunchbox granola bars (p. 66) and milk

As you become more involved in food and more aware of your own body's needs and demands, you are also going to become more conscious of food fads. Like the Hula-Hoop, new things come in big waves in this country and we all leap to attention—not very well informed but most enthusiastically and ready to jump on the bandwagon.

The latest craze in the nutrition circle is fiber, and every cereal advertised on television talks about the fiber content and many a bread has changed its old label to a new one giving fiber the big billing. Fiber is not a cure-all for anything though most experts agree we should perhaps eat more of it than we do.

On the kind of diet you are trying out here, you are bound to eat more fiber because whole grain cereals, dried beans and nuts, as well as fruits and vegetables contain a fair amount of it. Even without trying you'll be getting your fair share, so it is not necessary to sprinkle bran all over everything you eat.

GOLDEN GRAPEFRUIT

protein: 1 g   calories: 60

    1 large grapefruit
    2 tsp (10 ml) honey
    Grated rind of ½ orange

1.   Cut grapefruit in half crosswise. With the point of a serrated knife, cut around each small section of meat, separating it from the fiber. Take a kitchen scissors and cut out the center "spoke" of pith.
2.   Preheat the broiler.
3.   Place the grapefruit on a baking sheet and sprinkle each half with honey and orange rind.
4.   Place about 4 inches (10 cm) below broiler and broil until browned on the edges and bubbling.

Serve warm preferably in bowls because the heat will make the fruit very juicy.

Yield: 2 servings

COTTAGE CHEESE PANCAKES

protein: 9 g   calories: 280

1 cup (240 ml) cottage cheese
½ cup (120 ml) butter or margarine
2 eggs
1 cup (240 ml) unbleached flour
½ tsp (2.5 ml) baking powder
⅓ to ½ cup (80 to 120 ml) milk
¼ tsp (1.25 ml) salt

1. Put the cottage cheese and butter into a mixing bowl and beat together until creamy.
2. Break the eggs into the bowl, one at a time, and beat until well blended.
3. Add the flour mixed with the baking powder and beat in. Mix in the salt. Add the milk gradually, stirring, to make a thin batter but one that holds together when dropped from the end of the spoon.
4. Heat a lightly greased skillet or griddle and drop the batter in by spoonfuls. Cook on both sides, turning once.

   Serve with applesauce.

Yield: 4 to 6 servings

STRAWBERRY COOLER

protein: 11 g   calories: 225

    ½ cup (120 ml) strawberries
    1 cup (240 ml) milk
    1 tsp (5 ml) honey
    ½ tsp (2.5 ml) vanilla extract or ⅛ tsp (0.6 ml) almond extract
    1 tbsp (15 ml) dry milk powder

1.   Hull strawberries and place in blender container with remaining ingredients. Blend for 30 second until smooth, thick, and foamy.

Yield: 2 servings

NOODLE MUSHROOM CASSEROLE

protein: 14 g   calories: 325

  8 oz. (226.8 g) noodles
  ¼ lb. (113.4 g) mushrooms
  4 tbsp (60 ml) butter
  1 cup (240 ml) ricotta cheese
  ½ cup (120 ml) sour cream
  ½ cup (120 ml) grated Parmesan cheese
  Salt to taste
  Freshly ground pepper

1. Cook noodles according to package directions. Drain.
2. Meanwhile, slice mushrooms and sauté in butter for 5 minutes.
3. Mix mushrooms with ricotta cheese and sour cream in bowl. Season.
4. Butter a baking dish and layer half of noodles, half of mushroom mixture. Repeat.
5. Sprinkle with grated cheese.
6. Bake in a preheated 350°F (175°C) oven for 20 to 30 minutes.

Yield: 4 servings

WALDORF SALAD

protein: 4 g   calories: 450

This salad is named for a famous chef, Oscar of the Waldorf. You can play chef with it by adding whatever you like, such as grapes, carrots, bananas, or orange slices.

1 cup (240 ml) coarsely chopped celery
2 apples
½ cup (120 ml) mayonnaise
½ cup (120 ml) sour cream
1 tbsp (15 ml) lemon juice
½ tsp (2.5 ml) salt
Freshly ground pepper
1 tsp (5 ml) prepared mustard
½ cup (120 ml) chopped nuts

1. Chop celery coarsely. Chop unpeeled apples.
2. Mix together in a bowl the mayonnaise, sour cream, lemon juice, salt, pepper, and mustard.
3. Stir in celery, apples, nuts. Chill.

Yield: 4 servings

LEMON FREEZE

protein: 5 g   calories: 150

Butter
½ cup (120 ml) toasted wheat germ
½ cup (120 ml) toasted coconut
2 eggs, separated
⅔ cup (160 ml) sugar
Grated rind of 1 lemon
¼ cup (60 ml) lemon juice
⅔ cup (160 ml) nonfat dry milk
⅔ cup (160 ml) water

1. Lightly butter the bottom of a 9-inch (22.5-cm) cake pan.
2. Mix together the wheat germ and coconut and sprinkle one-third of the mixture in the bottom of the pan.
3. With a mixer, beat the egg yolks, gradually adding ½ cup (120 ml) of the sugar until the mixture is light and lemon-colored. Beat in the lemon rind and lemon juice.
4. In another bowl, put the egg whites, dry milk, water, and remaining sugar. Beat on highest speed until mixture is in stiff peaks. Depending on the power of your mixer, this can take up to 5 minutes.
5. Pour in the yolk mixture and blend together.
6. Pour half the mixture into the pan and sprinkle with one-third of the remaining wheat germ-coconut crumbs.
7. Pour in the remaining mixture and sprinkle remaining crumbs over the top.
8. Cover and freeze overnight. Remove from freezer 10 minutes before serving.

Yield: 8 servings

SATURDAY
total protein: 83 g
total calories: 2,326

BREAKFAST
the big baked apple
banana bread
milk

LUNCH
icy cucumber soup
honeyed cornbread
milk

DINNER
egg cheese puff
asparagus vinaigrette
100% bran muffins
yogurt pops
milk

Snack: buttermilk freeze

You are getting toward the end of your trial week and you may now call yourself a consumer in every sense of the word, especially if you have been doing the grocery shopping. It is in the markets that you can really see what goes on by reading labels, checking the condition of the vegetables, perhaps having to change the menu to fit what looks good that day. This is all part of the planning that goes into providing a balance of nutrition throughout the day—not just for one meal. Incidentally, following a balanced food regimen means no meal skipping because to make the nutrient puzzle come out right you have to fit all the pieces in their proper order, and that means three meals plus snacks.

Now is the time in your life to learn about that lifesaving subject called nutrition. Not only will you help yourself but, in a low-key way, you can include your family in on the act. Your mother would probably be delighted to have someone to help her with the cooking and the marketing—and the meal planning. This might be a time when two heads *are* better than one.

THE BIG BAKED APPLE

protein: 1 g   calories: 300

    1 big baking apple
    Raisins
    Brown sugar
    Butter
    Cinnamon
    Water, cider, or fruit juice

1.   With an apple corer, take out core from stem end almost to bottom of apple. With paring knife, peel off 1½ inches (3.75 cm) of skin around top.

2.   Alternately poke raisins, sugar, butter into hole, pushing down. Sprinkle cinnamon over top.

3.   Place a square of foil on a baking sheet. Put the apple on this and turn up the sides of the foil, making a cup. Pour some water, cider, or fruit juice into the cup around the base of the apple. This will help the apple cook from the bottom and keep it moist.

4.   Bake the apple for 35 to 45 minutes in a 350°F (175°C) oven until it is soft but not bursting.

5.   Cool slightly before eating.
    Serve with a dab of yogurt on top.

Yield: 1 serving

BANANA BREAD

protein: 3 g   calories: 215 (½ slice with a tbsp cream cheese)

½ cup (120 ml) butter or margarine
1 cup (240 ml) brown sugar
1 egg
1 cup (240 ml) unbleached white flour
½ cup (120 ml) whole wheat flour
1 tsp (5 ml) baking soda
½ tsp (2.5 ml) salt
2 large or 3 small bananas, mashed
¼ cup (60 ml) lemon yogurt
½ cup (120 ml) chopped nuts

1.   In bowl of electric mixer, beat together the butter and sugar until light and creamy.
2.   Beat in the egg.
3.   Mix together the flours, baking soda, and salt.
4.   Combine the bananas and yogurt in a small bowl.
5.   Add the flour mixture to the butter and sugar alternately with the banana mixture, beating well.
6.   Stir in nuts.
7.   Turn batter into a greased 9-by-5-inch (22.5-by-12.5-cm) loaf pan. Bake in a preheated 350°F (175°C) oven 50 to 60 minutes until bread tests done.
8.   Turn out of pan onto rack and cool before slicing.

Yield: 1 loaf

Note: To test if a cake or bread is done, stick a cake straw or broom straw into the center. If it comes out clean, with no wet batter on it, the cake is done.

ICY CUCUMBER SOUP

protein: 3 g   calories: 190

> 3 medium-sized cucumbers
> 1 tbsp (15 ml) salt
> 1 cup (240 ml) lemon yogurt or 1 cup plain yogurt and 1
>   tbsp (15 ml) lemon juice
> 2 ice cubes
> ½ cup (120 ml) water
> 1 tbsp (15 ml) fresh dill or 1 tsp (5 ml) dried dill
> Salt to taste
> Freshly ground pepper
> Chopped chives

1. Peel cucumbers. Cut them in half lengthwise and with a spoon scrape out the seeds. Dice the cucumbers and put in a bowl. Sprinkle with 1 tbsp salt (15 ml). Let stand for 30 minutes. Drain well.

2. Place cucumbers, yogurt, ice cubes, and water in blender. Blend well. Stir in dill and salt and pepper to taste. Chill.

   Serve with chopped chives on top.

Yield: 4 servings

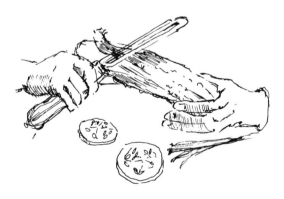

HONEYED CORNBREAD

protein: 5 g   calories: 190

1 cup (240 ml) yellow cornmeal
¾ cup (180 ml) flour
¼ cup (60 ml) wheat germ
3 tsp (15 ml) baking powder
½ tsp (2.5 ml) salt
2 eggs
1 cup (240 ml) milk
2 tbsp (30 ml) honey
¼ cup (60 ml) melted shortening

1. Put cornmeal, flour, wheat germ, baking powder, and salt into a large bowl.
2. Add the eggs, milk, honey, and shortening to the bowl, and with a wooden spoon, quickly mix everything together. Make sure all the dry ingredients are well moistened.
3. Turn the mixture into a well greased 9-inch (22.5-cm) square pan and bake in a preheated 400°F (200°C) oven for 30 minutes until golden.
   Serve warm.

Yield: 9 3-by-3-inch (7.5-by-7.5 cm) squares

EGG CHEESE PUFF

protein: 21 g   calories: 320

2 eggs
1½ oz. (42.52 g) cream cheese
¼ cup (60 ml) grated Swiss cheese
¼ cup (60 ml) milk
⅛ tsp (.6 ml) nutmeg
Salt to taste
Freshly ground pepper
Butter

1. Put all ingredients into blender and blend until smooth.
2. Butter a small baking dish and pour mixture into it.
3. Bake in preheated 400°F (200°C) oven for 20 minutes until puffy.

Yield: 1 serving

ASPARAGUS VINAIGRETTE

protein: 5 g   calories: 140

5 medium or 4 large stalks asparagus
Salt
Vinaigrette dressing (p. 21)
1 hard-boiled egg yolk
5 to 6 capers (optional)
1 tsp (5 ml) chopped chives (optional)

1. Using your hands, break off the bottoms of the asparagus stalks. They will want to break where they naturally should. With

a vegetable peeler, peel the stalks right up to the tips.

2.   Put the asparagus into a skillet large enough to hold them comfortably. Fill the skillet halfway up with cold water. Sprinkle in 1 tsp (5 ml) salt.

3.   Cover the pan and set it on high heat. Bring to a boil, turn the heat down to medium, and cook for 5 to 7 minutes until the very bottoms of the stalks can be pierced with a knife. Drain the asparagus and dry it on paper towels.

Serve it immediately or wait until it cools. In either case, pour about 1 tbsp (15 ml) of vinaigrette dressing over it. Sprinkle with egg yolk, capers, and chives.

Yield: 1 serving

100% BRAN MUFFINS

protein: 3 g   calories: 145 (1 muffin)

¾ cup (60 ml) buttermilk
1 cup (240 ml) 100% bran
1⅓ cups (320 ml) unbleached white flour
3 tsp (15 ml) baking powder
1 tsp (5 ml) salt
¼ cup (60 ml) melted shortening
½ cup (120 ml) brown sugar
1 egg

1.   Mix buttermilk and bran in small bowl.

2.   In large bowl combine flour, baking powder, and salt. Pour in shortening, sugar, and egg.

3.   Add bran mixture and mix quickly.

4.   Fill well-greased muffin tins two-thirds full.

5.   Bake for 25 minutes in a preheated 375°F (190°C) oven.

Yield: 12 muffins

YOGURT POPS

protein: 4 g   calories: 80

Here is another recipe for which you can use your imagination for flavorings. What other juice concentrates can you use with what other yogurts? Start thinking. Grape and cherry? Strawberry and lemon? Pineapple and . . . ?

   2 cups (480 ml) plain yogurt
   ½ small can frozen orange juice concentrate
   Grated rind of ½ orange
   Grated rind of 1 lemon

1.   Put all ingredients together in a bowl. Beat until well mixed.
2.   Spoon into small waxed paper cups. Set on a baking sheet and put into freezer. When pops are partially frozen, insert sticks (coffee stirrers or tongue depressors) into each one. To serve, cut off paper cup.

Yield: 10 pops

BUTTERMILK FREEZE

protein: 6 g   calories: 190

   1 cup (240 ml) crushed ice
   ½ cup (120 ml) buttermilk
   1 banana
   Juice of ½ lemon
   Sugar to taste

1.   Put all ingredients except sugar into blender. Blend until foamy. Add sugar to taste.

Yield: 1 serving

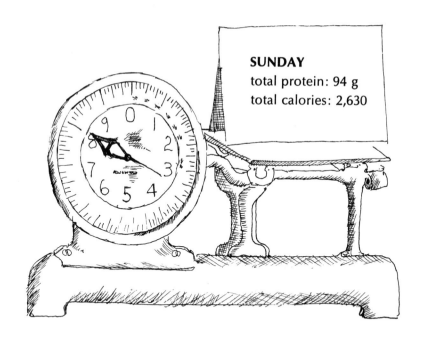

SUNDAY
total protein: 94 g
total calories: 2,630

BREAKFAST
1 egg scrambled in 1 tsp butter with 1 tsp grated orange rind
banana bake
cheese popovers
milk

LUNCH
peanut soup
crunchy coleslaw
milk

DINNER
special cheese fondue with bread sticks and apples
jolly green salad
fresh fruit

Snack: glass of milk and 2 almond-cream-cheese cookies

This is your last day of exam week in the vegetarian meal
course. How do you feel? We would be willing to bet that you

haven't missed animal protein nearly as much as you thought you would—and you've already discovered that there are a lot of very interesting foods around that you haven't tried before. If you want to continue for another week, or more, take the recipes and plan a week of your own. Or take the week you've just done and substitute comparable dishes until you really feel that you can go it on your own. If you are taking a course in home economics, discuss all this with your teacher. She will be able to answer a lot of the questions you might have and will probably be able to give you some good ideas. She might even let you tell the class about it. How's that for extra points?

BANANA BAKE

---

protein: 3 g   calories: 260

An underripe banana is one with no brown spots on the skin. It is not at all soft and may even have a little green on it. These are best for cooking because they don't go mushy.

4 underripe bananas
2 tbsp (30 ml) butter or margarine
2 tbsp (30 ml) honey or brown sugar
1 cup (240 ml) orange juice
¼ cup (60 ml) chopped almonds (optional)

1.   Peel bananas and cut in half lengthwise. Place in buttered baking dish.
2.   Heat together the butter, honey, and orange juice. Pour over the bananas.
3.   Bake in a preheated 350°F (175°C) oven for 20 minutes, basting occasionally.
4.   Sprinkle with chopped almonds, if you wish.

Yield: 4 servings

CHEESE POPOVERS

protein: 9 g   calories: 200

2 eggs
1 cup (240 ml) unbleached white flour
1 cup (240 ml) milk
½ tsp (2.5 ml) salt
2 tbsp (30 ml) finely grated Parmesan cheese
Butter

1. Put all ingredients into blender or bowl of mixer and blend or beat until batter is smooth.
2. Butter 4 custard cups very heavily. Set the cups on a baking sheet. Fill each cup three-fourths full of batter.
3. Set in cold oven. Now they can stay indefinitely, overnight if you wish—refrigerated. When ready to bake, turn the oven to 450°F (230°C) and bake for 30 minutes. After about 25 minutes, check to see if popovers are getting too brown. If they are, turn the oven down to 400°F (200°C) and bake until they are crisp and airy.

Serve with lots of butter and strawberry jam.

Yield: 4 popovers

PEANUT SOUP

protein: 12 g   calories: 365

  2 tbsp (30 ml) butter or margarine
  1 medium-sized onion, chopped
  1 stalk of celery, chopped
  1 tbsp (15 ml) unbleached white flour
  4 cups (960 ml) vegetable broth
  ½ cup (120 ml) smooth peanut butter
  1 cup (240 ml) half-and-half
  Chopped peanuts

1.   Heat butter in saucepan and sauté onion and celery until soft, but not brown.
2.   Stir in flour and cook for 2 minutes until blended.
3.   Add vegetable broth and, stirring constantly, bring to a boil over high heat.
4.   Remove from heat and pour half of soup into blender. Blend until smooth. Blend remaining half.
5.   Pour soup back into saucepan and add peanut butter and cream. Stir over low heat until smooth.
   Serve garnished with peanuts.

Yield: 4 servings

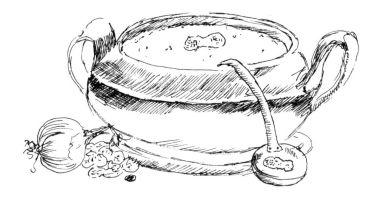

CRUNCHY COLESLAW

protein: 5 g   calories: 120

      2 cups (480 ml) shredded cabbage
      1 cup (240 ml) shredded carrots
      ½ cup (120 ml) raisins
      ½ cup (120 ml) toasted sunflower seeds
      ¼ cup (60 ml) buttermilk
      ½ cup (120 ml) cottage cheese
      1 tsp (5 ml) vinegar
      2 tsp (10 ml) sugar

1.   Mix cabbage, carrots, raisins, and sunflower seeds together in a bowl.
2.   In blender put buttermilk, cottage cheese, vinegar, and sugar. Blend until smooth.
3.   Toss vegetables with dressing. Refrigerate.

Yield: 5 servings

SPECIAL CHEESE FONDUE

protein: 20 g   calories: 315

This is a dish to be enjoyed with your parents. It does have wine in it, but the alcohol cooks away and you will probably not notice any particular wine flavor. The reason for adding wine instead of, say, milk is to make the cheese the proper thickness for dunking.

    1 clove garlic
    ½ lb. (226.8 g) Swiss Gruyère cheese in one piece
    ½ lb. (226.8 g) Cheddar cheese in one piece
    2 tbsp (30 ml) cornstarch
    1½ cups (360 ml) dry white wine
    1 tbsp (15 ml) lemon juice
    ⅛ tsp (.6 ml) grated nutmeg
    French bread
    3 Cortland apples

To make this dish, you should use an earthenware pot with a heatproof bottom. You can start it on the stove and then transfer the pot to a Sterno or alcohol burner for serving.

1. Peel the clove of garlic and cut it in half. Rub the inside of the pot with the cut pieces of garlic.
2. Cut the cheeses into small cubes and toss them with the cornstarch in a bowl.
3. Pour the wine into the pot and set it over medium heat on the stove. When small bubbles begin to form, put in the cubes of cheese, about ½ cup at a time. Stir constantly with a wooden spoon. You do not want the cheese to lump, which it will do if it goes into the wine too fast or gets too hot. It will take awhile to get all the cheese melted, so don't give up. When the cheese is all melted, stir in the lemon juice and nutmeg.

4.   Transfer the pot to an alcohol burner in the middle of the dining table.

5.   Meanwhile, have someone cut up lots of cubes of French bread and lots of apple slices, and put them in bowls or baskets.

6.   Each person needs one long fork for dunking and one regular fork for eating. Spear the bread cubes and the apples on the long fork and dip into the cheese fondue. The cheese will be stringy, so just wind it up as you go.

Yield: 4 to 5 servings

Note: The cheese should not come to a boil.

Whoever loses a piece of bread in the pot has to pay a forfeit, usually a kiss for everyone at the table!

JOLLY GREEN SALAD

protein: 4 g   calories: 165

1 head leaf lettuce
½ cup (120 ml) cooked lima beans
½ cup (120 ml) cooked green peas
½ cup (120 ml) chopped raw zucchini
2 cups (480 ml) fresh spinach leaves
Green giant dressing

1.   Tear lettuce into medium-sized pieces and put in bowl with beans, peas, spinach, and zucchini.
2.   Toss with dressing.

Yield: 4 servings

GREEN GIANT DRESSING

protein: 2 g   calories: 210

½ cup (120 ml) mayonnaise
¼ cup (60 ml) yogurt
2 tbsp (30 ml) vinegar
¼ cup (60 ml) chopped parsley
2 tbsp (30 ml) chopped chives
½ cup (120 ml) spinach leaves
½ tsp (2.5 ml) salt
Freshly ground pepper

1.   Combine all ingredients in blender and blend until smooth. Refrigerate and use on salad, baked tomato halves, as a dip for raw vegetables.

Yield: 4 servings

SUPER SNACKS— AND SANDWICHES

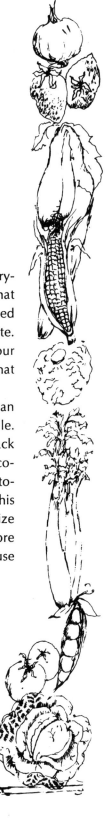

Have you ever noticed that after a while all the factory-produced snack foods begin to taste the same—no matter what the names happen to be? Heavy on the salt and oil, color-shaded from pale tan to deep orange, and with a bit of a cottony taste. We guarantee that you won't get any of these features in our snacks, and we certainly don't know the secret behind that bright-orange color!

It's fun to think up names for new fast foods and if you can think up a new combination, you can give it a zippy handle. Here's a good idea for a party: Put out bowls or baskets of snack material—sunflower seeds, pumpkin seeds, raisins, peanuts, coconut, cereals, popcorn, dried fruit—and let your friends put together whatever appeals to them. Each person has to name his or her own concoction. Have a panel of judges and give a prize to the best-tasting and best-named snack. The health food store may be a good place to shop for the basic materials because you can buy in bulk and save money.

Now, some snack recipes. The sandwiches come later.

SEED-NUT BRITTLE

protein: 2 g   calories: 80 (one piece)

Nuts and seeds are important to a vegetable diet for many reasons. One, they add variety. Two, they add texture and chewiness. Three, they are good sources of protein, calcium, fats, and vitamin B_6. Think about seeds as they really are—the beginning of all life and the storage warehouse for life-giving nutrients.

Milk is a good complementary protein for this food group, so you might get into the habit of drinking a glass of it whenever you eat anything made of beans, nuts, or seeds. When you think about it, it's really hard to find anything better than a peanut butter sandwich on whole wheat bread with a glass of cold milk. Or try this brittle between meals, again with a glass of milk.

    2 cups (480 ml) sugar
    1 cup (240 ml) raw peanuts
    1 cup (240 ml) pumpkin seeds
    1 tsp (5 ml) vanilla

1.   Pour sugar into heavy iron skillet. Set on medium heat and let cook until sugar burns brown and forms a golden syrup. Do not stir; just shake the pan from time to time. Be sure to wear potholder gloves when doing this. Sugar can cause very painful burns.
2.   When sugar has turned to syrup, remove skillet from heat and stir in vanilla, seeds and peanuts. Pour mixture onto a buttered cookie sheet or a piece of aluminum foil. Do not try to get the last bits out of the pan.
3.   Put the skillet in the sink and run very hot water into it.
4.   Let brittle cool; then break into pieces.

Yield: 8 servings

SHORTSTOP SNACKS

All dried fruits are high in fiber. They are also good sources of vitamin A, iron, and potassium. Couple them with extra protein and you've got an easy high-energy item. Dates and prunes are naturals for stuffing with nuts, cheese, or other fruits.

2 dates stuffed with sharp Cheddar or cottage cheese
    protein: 4 g, calories: 100
2 dates stuffed with 2 tsp (10 ml) peanut butter
    protein: 2½ g, calories: 100
2 dates stuffed with 2 pecans
    protein: ½ g, calories: 60
2 dates stuffed with 2 almonds
    protein: ¾ g, calories: 60
2 dates stuffed with 2 tsp (10 ml) raisins
    protein: ½ g, calories: 60

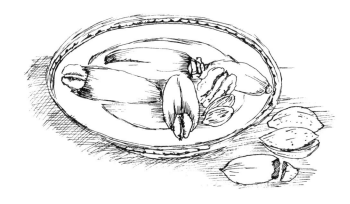

LUNCHBOX GRANOLA BARS

protein: 3 g   calories: 200 (1 piece)
protein: 3 g   calories: 210 (with wheat germ and dried milk)

    3 eggs
    1 cup (240 ml) brown sugar
    ¼ cup (60 ml) melted butter
    ½ cup (120 ml) unbleached white flour
    ½ tsp (2.5 ml) salt
    2½ cups (600 ml) granola cereal
    1 tsp (5 ml) vanilla

1.   In mixing bowl beat eggs until foamy. Pour in sugar and beat until light. Stir in melted butter.
2.   Beat in flour, salt, and granola. Add vanilla. Mix well.
3.   Grease a 9-by-9-inch (22.5-by-22.5-cm) square pan and pour batter into it.
4.   Bake for 30 minutes in a preheated 350°F (175°C) oven until firm and lightly browned.
5.   Cut into squares while warm and remove to rack to cool.

Yield: 24 bars

These are good for a quick dessert with ice cream or whipped cream.

If you want to be inventive, add 2 tbsp (30 ml) each wheat germ and nonfat dry milk, or ¼ cup (60 ml) sesame seeds and 1 tbsp (15 ml) grated orange rind.

THREE-WAY COMBO

protein: 8 g   calories: 270

Popcorn is a good source of fiber and a relatively low-calorie food. But it is also low in protein, so to make a healthy combination of crunchy snack foods, try mixing popcorn with peanuts and shredded wheat. Add cheese for extra zip.

4 cups (960 ml) popped corn
2 cups (480 ml) bite-sized shredded wheat
1 cup (240 ml) raw peanuts
2 tbsp (30 ml) butter or margarine
2 tbsp (30 ml) oil
1 small clove garlic
1 tsp (5 ml) salt
2 tbsp (30 ml) grated Parmesan cheese

1.   Put popcorn into large bowl. Cut bite-sized shredded wheat biscuits in half and add to bowl. Mix in peanuts.
2.   Heat butter and oil together until butter is melted. Put garlic clove through a garlic press and add to the butter.
3.   Pour garlic butter over mixture in bowl and stir well.
4.   Sprinkle salt and cheese in and stir again, so all is well mixed.
5.   Spread mixture on cookie sheet and bake at 300°F (150°C) for 30 minutes, stirring occasionally.

Yield: 8 servings

SNACK PACK

protein: 1.5 g   calories: 150

1 15-oz. (425.25 g) package mixed dried fruit
½ cup (120 ml) *each* golden and dark raisins
½ cup (120 ml) shredded coconut
¼ cup (60 ml) toasted sunflower seeds

1.   Chop the dried fruit into fairly small pieces. Put all ingredients into a bowl and mix together. Pack in small amounts in plastic bags. Tie tightly and take along on bike hikes, camping trips, and other energetic activities.

Yield: 4 servings

ALMOND CREAM-CHEESE COOKIES

protein: 1½ g   calories: 145 (1 cookie)

Almonds have a lot of calcium and iron. We're adding the dry milk for protein and the cream cheese for texture. The rest is just for fun.

¾ cup (180 ml) butter or margarine
1⅓ cups (320 ml) brown sugar, packed
2 eggs
1 cup (240 ml) unbleached white flour
2 tbsp (30 ml) dry skim milk
¾ tsp (3.7 ml) baking soda
½ tsp (2.5 ml) salt
1 tsp (5 ml) almond extract
1 cup (240 ml) *each* slivered toasted almonds, oats, raisins
Softened cream cheese

1.   In mixing bowl cream together the butter and sugar until light and smooth. Beat in eggs, one at a time.
2.   Mix together the flour, dry milk, baking soda, and salt.
3.   Beat into butter mixture. Add almond extract. Stir in almonds, oats, and raisins, mixing well.
4.   Grease a cookie sheet.
5.   Drop batter by spoonfuls onto sheet, about 2 inches (5 cm) apart.
6.   Bake in a preheated 350°F (175°C) oven for 12 to 14 minutes. Remove from cookie sheet with spatula.

Yield: 3 dozen cookies

While cookies are warm you can spread them with cream cheese and bend them in half, making a half-moon shape. Or you can leave them round and spread them with cream cheese and top with another round, making sandwiches. Cool and refrigerate.

LET'S OPEN-FACE IT

Where would we be without the sandwich? It's the answer to the picnic, the party, the patio lunch, the soup or salad supper. Sandwiches can be made out of anything and everything and you don't necessarily need bread. Many of the sandwiches we're suggesting here can be made without the top slice of bread, if you're worried about calories—and who isn't, at least some of the time? We've also got an eggplant sandwich and a sandwich that is best after it's been sat on for a while. And if you automatically think "ham and cheese"—don't. That's out and the crunchy veg is in.

We're going to suggest a lot of different sandwich spreads with the thought that you might like to use them for a party. Put the different spreads and ingredients, such as bean sprouts, into brightly colored bowls, arrange the breads in baskets, and have glass flowerpots filled with ice and sticks of celery, carrots, and zucchini.

1. finely grated carrots mixed with softened cream cheese and a bit of ground ginger on raisin bread
2. grated Swiss cheese mixed with catsup and chopped raw spinach leaves on rye
3. curried egg salad and avocado slices on whole wheat
4. grated zucchini mixed with egg salad on white
5. chopped celery and peanut butter on graham crackers
6. bean sprouts, cream cheese, and sliced tomato
7. cream cheese mixed with sesame seeds and cucumber slices

Now for the breadless sandwich:

Romaine lettuce has a lot going for it as it has more vitamins than many of the other lettuces, more flavor, and more crunch. It also has a shape that makes it perfect for sandwiches. Just spread filling down the middle of the leaf, fold it up and eat it.

A SANDWICH TO SIT ON

protein: 6 g   calories: 240

1.   Take a round crusty roll, with sesame seeds if you wish. Cut it open and pour a little French vinaigrette dressing on both sides. Don't soak it, just wet it a bit.
2.   Fill the roll with slices of raw mushroom, slices of tomato, lettuce, slices of artichoke hearts, and hard-boiled eggs. Wrap it up, put it on a plate, and put something heavy on top of it— like a brick or a heavy can. Just let it stand for a couple of hours or half a day. Or you could put it at the bottom of your knapsack or bicycle bag if you wish. Or sit on it. Just so it gets all pressed together for a length of time.

You can vary the ingredients as long as you put dressing on the roll. That's the basic rule for this kind of sandwich. You could even make a big long one, like a hero, and slice it into individual servings after it has been weighted.

EGGPLANT SANDWICH

protein: 7 g   calories: 290

    1 egg
    2 tbsp (30 ml) milk
    Seasoned bread crumbs
    Mild Cheddar or Monterey Jack cheese
    1 eggplant, peeled and cut into slices
    Oil

1.   Beat the egg with the milk.
2.   Have ready two bowls, one filled with bread crumbs, the other with the egg mixture.
3.   Cut slices of cheese about the same shape as the eggplant slices.
4.   Sandwich cheese between slices of eggplant.
5.   Dip these sandwiches into the egg mixture, then into the crumbs, coating both sides well.
6.   Heat oil in a large skillet. When the oil is hot, sauté the eggplant rounds until golden on both sides and the cheese has melted.

    Serve hot with mustard and pickles.

Yield: 6 servings

THE BEAUTIFUL SOUPS AND SALADS

Soup can be a main course for breakfast, lunch, or dinner. Don't laugh—we do mean breakfast. Soup can contain a large amount of the day's protein requirement and a lot of other minerals and vitamins besides. On a really hot summer morning when you don't feel like eating anything—but you should—try a cup of icy-cold blueberry-apple soup. Or to reverse the weather picture—get out of that nice warm bed when there's ice on the *inside* of the windows and have a warming bowl of Cheddar cheese soup with a toasted bran muffin (with honey).

We don't suggest soup three times a day, but there are so many souper possibilities that three times a week is hardly enough. Soups can be like stews or they can be like salads. Thick or thin, hot or cold, they are full of good things.

SOME LIKE IT HOT

There is a great temptation to make soup the whole meal when you are trying out a vegetarian diet. Don't. It is possible to incorporate everything you need nutritionally into one soup, but it does not make a very interesting meal. After you finish a large bowl of whatever kind it might be, you are left with a

Is-that-all? feeling—definitely not a good attitude to have because it just leads to fingers in the peanut butter. If a soup, such
as mushroom-barley or corn and cheese, turns out to be the
main course, supplement it with salad or raw vegetable sticks,
bread or muffins, cheese and fruit, or a custard dessert. Then
you really know you've eaten a meal.

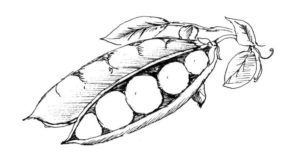

GREAT GARDEN PEA SOUP

protein: 7 g   calories: 105 (with milk)

Peas are a good source of protein, especially raw, and if
you're a gardener you know how good they can taste right off
the vine. If you don't grow your own, beg some from a neighbor
who does, because there's nothing better in early summer than
fresh peas in soup or salad or just plain.

2 lbs. (.91 kg) fresh peas
4 scallions, white part only
4 cups (960 ml) vegetable broth
1 cup (240 ml) cream or milk
Salt to taste
Freshly ground pepper
Chopped chives

1. Shell the peas and put them into a saucepan with 4 to 5
clean pods.

2. Chop the white part of the scallions and add to the pot with the broth. Bring to a boil, cover, and simmer until peas are tender, about 10 minutes.

3. Pour into blender container and blend until smooth.

4. Return to saucepan and add cream or milk. Salt and pepper to taste. Reheat and serve sprinkled with chives.

Yield: 4 servings

Note: Green tops of scallions can be chopped fine and used as chives.

CORN AND CHEESE CHOWDER

---

protein: 15 g   calories: 320

2 tbsp (30 ml) butter
1 tbsp (15 ml) oil
1 medium-sized onion
½ cup (120 ml) chopped celery
3 cups (720 ml) cooked potatoes, diced
2 cups (480 ml) milk
2 cups (480 ml) cream-style corn
2 cups (480 ml) shredded Cheddar cheese
Chopped parsley

1. In a heavy saucepan heat butter and oil. Sauté onion and celery over medium heat until soft. Add potatoes, milk, and corn. Cook, stirring, until very hot. Remove from heat and stir in cheese. When cheese is melted, serve soup with parsley on top.

Yield: 6 servings

Note: If you are using new potatoes, why don't you leave the skins on? There is a lot of good nutrient in a potato skin and they also add flavor—if well scrubbed, that is.

SOME LIKE IT COLD

Cold but not freezing. The flavor disappears when food is too cold, so if you're very hot and thirsty, drink a glass of ice water, which is the best thirst-quencher anyway, and save the soup until you cool down a bit.

GAZPACHO

---

protein: 5 g   calories: 230

This soup is correctly called a liquid salad, and in addition to everything else, it is full of garden sunshine. There are many ways of making gazpacho and one of the easiest is simply to put the vegetables through the blender. But, one thing you may miss on a vegetarian diet is chewing, so we suggest chopping all of the ingredients. If you are really pressed for time, you could put most of the vegetables in the blender and leave out small amounts of chopped vegetables to sprinkle on top.

3 cucumbers
3 tomatoes
1 onion
1 clove garlic
1 green pepper
4 cups (960 ml) tomato juice
Salt to taste
Freshly ground pepper
Juice of 1 lemon
6 tbsp (90 ml) oil
¼ cup (60 ml) chopped almonds

1.   Peel cucumbers and tomatoes and chop fine. Put into large bowl. Peel onion and garlic and chop fine. Add to bowl. Seed

pepper, chop fine, and add to bowl. Stir in tomato juice. Season to taste. Stir in lemon juice and oil.

2. Chill.

3. Before serving, stir in almonds.

Yield: 6 servings

CURRIED ZUCCHINI SOUP

protein: 2 g   calories: 45 (with milk)

Zucchini is another one of nature's perfect foods and, raw or cooked, it's delicious in a lot of different ways. It is very low in calories and should be eaten with the skin on.

3 small zucchini, unpeeled
1 small onion
1 clove garlic
4 cups (960 ml) vegetable broth
1 cup (240 ml) milk or light cream
Salt to taste
Freshly ground pepper
Curry powder to taste

1. Slice zucchini into rounds and put in heavy saucepan. Peel onion and garlic and chop fine. Add to pan. Pour in vegetable broth and bring to a boil.

2. Cover pan and simmer for 15 minutes until vegetables are soft.

3. Put mixture in blender, 2 cups (480 ml) at a time, and blend smooth.

4. Add milk and season to taste. Pour into a pitcher and chill.

Yield: 6 servings

BLUEBERRY-APPLE SOUP

protein: ¾ g   calories: 165
protein: 1½ g   calories: 175 (with yogurt)

Apples are good for us, or so we've always been told. Mythology would have us believe they have miraculous healing powers. It is true that an apple will soothe an upset stomach, so try one when you're feeling a bit edgy or your stomach isn't quite all there. It's good medicine that is very pleasant to take.

Combined with blueberries and yogurt, apple juice can make a very tasty cold soup.

> 2 cups (480 ml) blueberries (fresh or frozen)
> 4 cups (960 ml) apple juice
> Lemon yogurt

1. Put blueberries in blender with apple juice. Blend until smooth. Chill. Strain if you wish before serving.
2. Put a spoonful of yogurt in each cup of soup.

Yield: 4 servings

Note: You can vary this by using cranberry-apple juice.

THE SLIMMING SALADS

Speaking of salads, here we will put in a pitch for you to "grow your own." The green that grows in your backyard garden, watched over by you with a lot of tender, loving care, is bound to have more beneficial nutrients than the greens that "grow" in the supermarket under hot lights and plastic wrap.

Even in our northern states, it is possible to cultivate successfully a small garden of the vegetables you like best—and are best for you. Try some lettuces, tomatoes, green beans, one or two zucchini plants, a green pepper or two, and cucumbers. You can put cucumbers up on a trellis and grow them vertically to save space.

As this is really not a gardening book, we'll leave it at that and merely add that, for winter gardening, nothing beats sprouting, which takes up no space at all and is a super way of getting crunchy vitamins all winter long—even in the deep dark of the city.

As we keep telling you, there is nothing like the leafy dark greens and deep yellow vegetables for iron, vitamins, and minerals. So always include a few leaves of spinach, cress, romaine, cabbage, or chard in your salads.

Which brings us to the subject of appearance. We've all eaten meals that are completely blah in looks—the most famous being an all-white plate of fish, potatoes, and cauliflower—which kills your appetite right away. The leafy greens add color and design to your salad, and it is fun to experiment with different vegetables and see what you can come up with.

Texture is another selling point in salads and if you combine the greens with some dried foods, such as seeds or beans, you will get contrast of texture as well as a good combination of vitamins, amino acids, and minerals. Seeds and nuts add extra protein—and crunch.

Use seasonal vegetables for economy and freshness. In the winter try combining celery root, turnips, or carrots with watercress, spinach, and scallions for green.

Ideally, you should prepare a salad at the last minute, but if you do fix it ahead, be sure to refrigerate it because vitamins disappear fast when a salad is left at room temperature.

The salads we are suggesting are not whole meals in themselves. They need the addition of other vegetables and dairy products to round out their nutritional value, but they can be substituted for any of the salads we've included in the week's menu plan.

CAESAR AUGUSTUS SALAD

protein: 7 g   calories: 180

   1 head romaine lettuce
   8-oz. can (226.8 g) asparagus tips, drained and dried
   1 clove garlic
   1 tsp (5 ml) dry mustard
   ½ tsp (2.5 ml) salt
   Freshly ground pepper
   1 tbsp (15 ml) lemon juice
   3 tbsp (45 ml) oil
   1 egg
   ¼ cup (60 ml) grated Parmesan cheese
   2 tbsp (30 ml) shelled pistachio nuts
      or same amount of pine nuts

1.   Wash and dry lettuce leaves thoroughly. Tear into pieces and put in large bowl. Add asparagus tips.
2.   Chop the garlic fine and mix it with the mustard and salt in a small bowl. Add some pepper, the lemon juice, and the oil and stir all together until well blended.
3.   Break the egg over the salad greens and pour on the dressing. Toss all together, mixing well.
4.   Add the cheese and nuts and toss again.
Serve immediately.

Yield: 4 servings

   You can add ½ cup of croutons (120 ml) if you wish or substitute sunflower seeds for the nuts.

LENTIL SALAD

protein: 16 g   calories: 320

    2 cups (480 ml) lentils
    Water
    1 onion stuck with 2 cloves
    1 stalk celery
    1 bay leaf
    ½ tsp (2.5 ml) thyme
    4 scallions, chopped
    Vinaigrette dressing
    Salt
    Freshly ground pepper
    2 ripe tomatoes or 1 cup (240 ml) canned Italian tomatoes
    2 tbsp (30 ml) minced parsley

1. Put lentils into large pot and add water to cover.
2. Add onion, celery, bay leaf, and thyme. Bring to a boil, cover, and cook for 20 to 30 minutes until tender but not mushy.
3. Drain and remove vegetables and herbs.
4. Turn lentils into a bowl and add just enough dressing to moisten lentils. Do not soak. Season to taste with salt and pepper. Cover and chill for 2 to 3 hours.
5. At serving time, peel and chop ripe tomatoes or drain and chop canned tomatoes and mix into lentils. Sprinkle with parsley.

Yield: 6 servings

THE BIG BEAN SALAD

protein: 5 g   calories: 145

½ lb. (226.8 g) fresh green beans
½ cup (120 ml) bean sprouts
½ green pepper, chopped
3 scallions, chopped
2 cups (480 ml) spinach leaves
2 cups (480 ml) leaf lettuce leaves
Green herb dressing

1. Cut green beans into ½-inch (1.25-cm) pieces and cook in a large amount of boiling salted water until just tender—5 to 7 minutes.
2. Drain beans and run under cold water until they are cool. Dry on paper towels.
3. Put all ingredients into large bowl and toss with green herb dressing.

Yield: 3 servings

GREEN HERB DRESSING

6 tbsp (90 ml) yogurt
3 tbsp (45 ml) mayonnaise
3 tbsp (45 ml) cottage cheese
1 tsp (5 ml) celery seed
2 tbsp (30 ml) chopped parsley
1 tbsp (15 ml) chopped chives
2 sprigs fresh dill weed
Salt to taste

1. Put all ingredients into container of blender and blend until smooth. Season to taste.

Yield: 3 servings

THE UNNECESSARY POTATO FAMINE

Now is the time to have a serious word about potatoes. They are the most talked-against vegetable just because someone once said that potatoes are fattening. They are not—it is the additives in the form of butter and sour cream that are fattening. Potatoes have everything going for them. Just listen!

- A medium-sized potato with the skin has one-quarter as much vitamin C as an orange.
- The average-sized potato has only 100 calories, which is equal to one pear, one large apple, a banana, or two slices of bacon.
- An average potato has three grams of protein, one to two times more than the average slice of bread.
- Milk and cheese complement the protein in potato, so a potato topped with cottage cheese and chives or yogurt, or a cream of potato soup, are naturals.
- There is a lot of nutritive value in the potato skin, so you should at least cook them with their skins on. Then you can peel or not as you wish.

Do you want to try a wonderful lo-cal baked potato? Just put a baking potato in the oven at 350°F (175°C) and leave it for 2 hours. When you slit it open, it will be all fluffy and will *not* need any butter—just salt and pepper. Eat it, skin and all. Have we convinced you that you can eat a potato now and then—or more often than that?

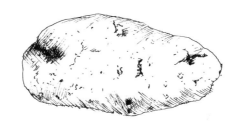

POTATO-MUSHROOM SALAD

protein: 4 g   calories: 290

5 large potatoes, unpeeled
Salt to taste
Freshly ground pepper
French dressing
½ lb. (226.8 g) mushrooms
3 tbsp (45 ml) chopped chives
½ cup (120 ml) finely chopped scallions or onions
¼ cup (60 ml) chopped parsley

1.   Put potatoes in a large pot and cover with cold water. Cover the pot, bring to a boil, and cook over medium heat until potatoes are tender when pierced with a fork in the thickest part.
2.   Drain potatoes and peel as soon as you can handle them.
3.   Dice into bite-sized pieces and put into a bowl. Season with salt and pepper and pour on enough French dressing to coat the potatoes lightly. There should not be any dressing sitting in the bottom of the bowl.
4.   Let stand until cool.
5.   Before serving, slice mushrooms thinly.
6.   Gently mix in chives, onion, parsley, and mushrooms.
    Serve on fresh greens.

Yield: 6 servings

Note: Because this does not have any mayonnaise, it is lower in calories and also can be left sitting on the counter while it is cooling.

TABBOULI

protein: 7.5 g   calories: 330

This salad has a wonderful name to drop around and it makes use of one of our not too often used grains. Bulgur wheat is a good source of protein and can be served hot in pilaf as well as cold in salad. Try adding some ground sesame seed (tahini) to it to accent the already nutty flavor.

2 cups (480 ml) vegetable broth
½ tsp (2.5 ml) salt
1 cup (240 ml) bulgur wheat
½ cup (120 ml) dried white beans, cooked
¼ cup (60 ml) chopped mint
2 cups (480 ml) chopped parsley
1 tomato, peeled and chopped
½ cup (120 ml) chopped onions or scallions
½ cup (120 ml) oil
¼ cup (60 ml) lemon juice

1. Put broth in saucepan with salt and bring to a boil.
2. Add bulgur wheat to pan, stirring into liquid.
3. Cover pan and set aside for 1 hour.
4. Fluff wheat with fork and turn into bowl.
5. Stir in all remaining ingredients and let stand for 2 hours.
   Serve on fresh greens.

Yield: 6 servings

THE HEARTY ENTRÉE

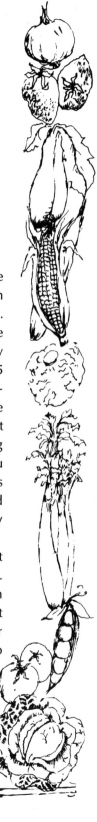

On a vegetarian diet there is a temptation to gorge on one big item—a salad with everything in it, an eggplant stuffed with cheese and other vegetables, an enormous blender concoction. No way—it doesn't take the place of a planned meal with more than one dish, which makes you sit down (important) and slowly and enjoyably eat food that will stick with you for the next 4 to 5 hours. Just for fun, some noontime make about 6 stuffed mushrooms. Put them on a plate with watercress and raw vegetable sticks. Take the plate to a table with a knife and fork and sit down. Eat the mushrooms slowly, cutting them up and stopping occasionally to really taste what you are eating. (Hopefully you have stuffed them with something you like.) See how long this meal stays with you, as compared to gulping down some food from the kitchen counter. Your attitude to the food you eat really does matter.

The main dish of a meal takes a bit of thought because it should be worked out with complementary protein in mind. Choose your protein food first—beans, cheese, eggs. Then fill in with the other foods that will make up a well-balanced meal. At the same time, try to keep color and texture at the top of your list because if food isn't appetizing, we tend not to eat it—no matter how good for us it may be.

We have tried to include some surprises as well as some fun dishes in these entrées. Remember that the protein grams and calories are counted for just one portion.

ROLL YOUR OWN

---

protein: 35 g   calories: 650

You are alone—and isn't it peaceful? We all need to be alone every now and then, just to think or dream or read a certain book or magazine, or perhaps write a poem or paint a picture. Here's an all-for-one dish that you can whip up in no time with perhaps a piece of carrot cake or corny apple pie for dessert—and always that glass of milk.

    2 eggs, separated
    1 tbsp (15 ml) flour
    Salt and pepper to taste
    ⅔ cup (160 ml) Ricotta cheese
    2 tbsp (30 ml) butter or margarine
    3 tbsp (45 ml) grated Parmesan cheese
    ¼ cup (60 ml) tomato sauce or yogurt

1.   Beat the yolks with the flour, salt, and pepper.
2.   Beat the whites until stiff and fold into the yolks.
3.   In a 9-inch (22.5-cm) skillet heat 1 tbsp (15 ml) butter. Pour the egg mixture into the skillet. Cook 4 minutes over medium-high heat.
4.   With the help of a spatula, slide the roll out onto a plate. Put the remaining tbsp (15 ml) of butter into the skillet and flip the roll back into the skillet to cook the other side.
5.   Fill the roll with the ricotta cheese. With the help of a spatula roll it up and slide it out onto a plate. Sprinkle with Parmesan cheese and tomato sauce or yogurt.

Yield: 1 serving

Note: The easiest way to fold egg whites into anything is with your hands, very gently using a scooping motion.

DOUBLE UP WITH CORN CREPES

protein: 3 g   calories: 90 (2 crepes)

In case you've never made crepes, now's the time to try. They're easy, fun, and great to build with. They will roll up, fold up, or stack. Cornmeal is a good source of protein and if you can find the stone-ground meal, so much the better. We're giving you one terrific way of using the crepes after you've made them. After that, it's up to you. They would be good for dessert with fresh fruit and fruit-flavored yogurt.

BASIC RECIPE

½ cup (120 ml) cornmeal
½ cup (120 ml) flour
1 tbsp (15 ml) melted butter or margarine
1 cup (240 ml) plus 2 tbsp (30 ml) milk
½ tsp (2.5 ml) salt
Freshly ground pepper
3 large eggs

1. Put all ingredients into blender or mixer and blend until smooth. Strain into a pitcher and refrigerate for 1 hour. Using a crepe pan, make thin crepes. Stack cooked crepes with a piece of waxed paper between each one. These can be frozen this way in a sealed plastic bag.

Yield: 24 crepes

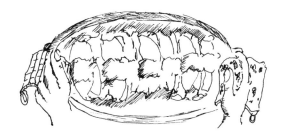

SPINACH-CHEESE FILLING

protein: 15 g   calories: 240

1 10-oz. (283.5 g) package chopped spinach
1 cup (240 ml) cottage cheese
2 eggs
½ cup (120 ml) grated Swiss cheese
½ tsp (2.5 ml) salt
Freshly ground pepper
1 tsp (5 ml) basil
1 tbsp (15 ml) minced parsley
12 corn crepes
2 cups (480 ml) tomato sauce
4 tbsp (60 ml) grated Mozzarella cheese

1. Cook spinach and drain well. Squeeze dry with hands.
2. Put cottage cheese, eggs, Swiss cheese, and spinach into large bowl. Mix together. Stir in salt, pepper, basil, and parsley.
3. Fill 12 crepes with this mixture, using about 2 tbsp (30 ml) per crepe. Spread mixture along center of crepe and roll up. Place filled crepes in bottom of greased baking dish in one layer. Pour tomato sauce over all and sprinkle with Mozzarella.
4. Bake in a preheated 325°F (160°C) oven for 20 minutes until heated through.

Serve with crunchy coleslaw and a fruit pie.

Yield: 6 servings

THE BEST OF THE ROOTS

protein: 4 g   calories: 240

This is a good casserole for a cold winter's night as it is warming to look at, to taste, and to smell cooking. Also, the vegetables are among those we see a lot of at that time of year, which means they will be less expensive. Serve baked onions with it and a salad of spinach and watercress with cottage cheese dressing.

3 sweet potatoes
2 medium parsnips
2 large carrots
2 tbsp (30 ml) butter or margarine
1 onion, chopped
2 tbsp (30 ml) unbleached white flour
1 cup (240 ml) orange juice
Salt to taste
Freshly ground pepper
½ tsp (2.5 ml) ground nutmeg
½ cup (120 ml) whole wheat bread crumbs
¼ cup (60 ml) toasted sesame seeds
2 tbsp (30 ml) butter or margarine

1.   Cook potatoes and parsnips in boiling water to cover until tender but not mushy. Cool, skin, and slice into rounds.
2.   Scrub carrots and slice into rounds. Cook in boiling salted water until tender. Drain and cool.
3.   In bottom of greased baking dish, layer carrots, potatoes, and parsnips.
4.   Heat 2 tbsp (30 ml) butter in saucepan and sauté onion until soft.
5.   Sprinkle flour over onion and cook, stirring, for 2 minutes. Pour orange juice into pan and cook, stirring, until thick and smooth. Season with salt, pepper, and nutmeg.

6. Pour sauce over vegetables in baking dish.

7. Mix crumbs and sesame seeds and sprinkle over top. Dot with butter.

8. Bake uncovered in a preheated 375°F (190°C) oven for 20 to 30 minutes until hot.

Yield: 6 servings

BEANY ROAST

protein: 15 g   calories: 230

We include this recipe just to prove to you that beans can be used in many, many ways and not taste the same each time. Lentils are among the most versatile—try sprouting them sometime. They're so crunchy you can eat them like peanuts.

1 cup (240 ml) lentils cooked according to package directions
1 cup (240 ml) grated cheese
2 tbsp (30 ml) chili sauce
3 eggs, beaten
2 tbsp (30 ml) minced parsley
1 tbsp (15 ml) grated onion
2 drops hot pepper sauce

1. Mix all ingredients together and turn into a flat baking dish.

2. Bake in a preheated 350°F (175°C) oven for 30 minutes until set.

Serve with tomato sauce, also with sliced cucumbers, Syrian bread, and a custard dessert.

Yield: 4 servings

ZUCCHINI EGG PUFF

protein: 12 g   calories: 180

We seem to keep pushing zucchini, but it has so much going for it as a vegetable, in bread, in cake, in soufflés, that it is hard to ignore. A most agreeable vegetable.

2 lbs. (.91 kg) zucchini, cut into rounds
2 tbsp (30 ml) bread crumbs
2 eggs, separated
½ 3-oz. (42.52 g) package cream cheese
½ cup (120 ml) grated Parmesan cheese
2 tbsp (30 ml) yogurt
½ tsp (2.5 ml) salt
Freshly ground pepper
½ tsp (2.5 ml) nutmeg
2 tbsp (30 ml) chopped chives

1.   Cook zucchini slices in boiling salted water until just tender—about 5 to 7 minutes. Drain and dry on paper towels.

2.   Grease a 9-inch (22.5-cm) pie plate and sprinkle bread crumbs over the bottom evenly.

3.   In the container of a blender put the egg yolks, cream cheese, Parmesan cheese, yogurt, salt, pepper, and nutmeg. Blend until smooth.

4.   Beat egg whites until stiff and fold into yolk mixture. Stir in chives.

5.   In pie plate put half of zucchini slices. Cover with half of egg mixture. Repeat ending with egg mixture on top.

6.   Bake in a preheated 350°F (175°C) oven for 30 minutes until golden and puffy.

Yield: 4 servings

PARTIES AND MORE PARTIES

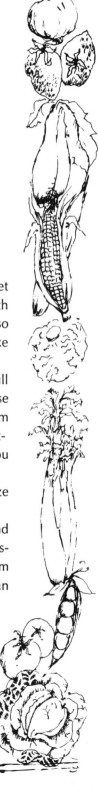

THE PLUPERFECT PIZZA PARTY

Invite ten friends for pizza and let them make their own. Set everything up beforehand on a table or the kitchen counter, with the ingredients in separate bowls. Provide small foil tart pans so they can make individual pizzas, and encourage everyone to make more than one kind so they can sample them all.

You might serve grape juice in wine glasses and baskets full of breadsticks. It would be less confusing if you and one close friend (who likes to cook) made all the crusts ahead, put them into the foil pans, and baked them. Then it's just a matter of putting in the fillings and baking again for a short time—while you have a game of bocce ball.

We'll be willing to bet that none of your guests will realize that this is a vegetarian meal.

Sharing with friends is a most important part of our lives and there is no reason not to make a party out of your new food discoveries. You are not trying to convert anyone—just giving them a lift with your new life and proving to yourself that a vegetarian diet does not have to be a lonely one.

Pizza Pizza

Zucchini Pizza

Nika's Potato Pizza

Apple Pie Pizza

PIZZA-PIZZA

---

protein: 4 g   calories: 125

1 1-lb. (.45 kg) loaf frozen white bread dough

1. Following directions on package of bread dough, shape crusts, and fill ten foil tart pans with dough.
2. Preheat oven to 500°F (260°C).
3. Bake on lowest rack of oven for 5 minutes until crust just starts to brown. Cool.

Yield: 10 crusts

ZUCCHINI PIZZA

protein: 4 g   calories: 55

    1 lb. (.45 kg) zucchini, unpeeled
    ½ cup (120 ml) shredded Mozzarella cheese
    ½ cup (120 ml) shredded Cheddar cheese
    1 egg
    Salt and pepper to taste

1.   Grate zucchini and squeeze with hands to get out moisture.
2.   Put zucchini in bowl and mix in cheeses and egg.
3.   With hands, make "crusts" of zucchini mixture in ten foil tart pans. Bake in a preheated 400°F (200°C) oven for 10 minutes.

Yield: 10 crusts

NIKA'S POTATO PIZZA

protein: 2 g   calories: 85

    2 cups (480 ml) mashed potatoes
    ¾ cup (180 ml) unbleached white flour
    ½ tsp (2.5 ml) salt
    Freshly ground pepper
    2 to 3 tbsp (30 to 45 ml) olive oil

1.   Mix potatoes with flour, salt, pepper, and oil. Work to a smooth dough. Pat dough into ten oiled tart pans. Do not leave any holes. Brush lightly with oil.
2.   Bake in a preheated 400°F (200°C) oven for 5 minutes.

Yield: 10 crusts

PIZZA FILLINGS

Put the following ingredients in separate bowls:

1 cup (240 ml) cubed mozzarella cheese
protein: 1 g   calories: 20

1 cup (240 ml) grated Parmesan cheese
protein: 2.5 g   calories: 30

1 cup (240 ml) chopped, drained canned tomatoes
protein: 0   calories: 4

1 cup (240 ml) spaghetti sauce
protein: 0   calories: 5

1 cup (240 ml) olives, sliced
protein: 0   calories: 10

1 cup (240 ml) sliced mushrooms
protein: 0   calories: 2

1 green pepper, cut into strips
protein: 0   calories: 2

2 onions, chopped
protein: 0   calories: 4

½ cup (120 ml) oil
protein: 0   calories: 120

Parsley, oregano, garlic salt

1. Preheat oven to 400°F (200°C).
2. Give each person some work space and let him or her create his or her own pizza, using whatever combinations appeal. Put the first ten pizzas on a baking sheet and bake for 15 to 20 minutes until the cheese is melted and bubbly. While eating the first batch, cook the second and so on.

APPLE PIE PIZZA FOR DESSERT

protein: 8 g   calories: 430

Double recipe of whole wheat pastry (p. 100)
1 1-lb. (.45 kg) can sliced pie apples
1 cup (240 ml) grated Cheddar cheese
1 cup (240 ml) raisins
1 cup (240 ml) chopped walnuts
1 cup (240 ml) brown sugar
Cinnamon

1.   Make and roll out pastry according to directions. Cut circles one inch (2.5 cm) larger than the outside rim of the foil tart pans. Lift the circles of pastry into the pans and press them down and around the top edges. Prick the bottoms and sides with a fork.
2.   Bake in a preheated 400°F (200°C) oven for 10 minutes. Cool.
3.   Put the sliced apples in a bowl. Put the cheese in another bowl. Mix together the raisins, nuts, and brown sugar and put in a bowl.
4.   To put a tart together, you sprinkle cheese over the bottom. Fill almost to the top with apples. Sprinkle the raisin mixture over the apples, covering the top.
5.   Bake at 400°F (200°C) for 30 minutes.

Yield: 10 servings

Note: Make sure you put the tart pans on a baking sheet as they will probably drip over.

WHOLE WHEAT PASTRY

1 cup (240 ml) whole wheat flour
2 tbsp (30 ml) brown sugar
½ cup (120 ml) rolled oats
½ cup (120 ml) butter
1 egg yolk

In large bowl combine flour, sugar and oats. Add butter cut in pieces and work with fingers until dough is crumbly. Stir in egg yolk and work dough until it becomes a smooth, noncrumbly ball. Flatten and wrap in plastic wrap. Chill. This makes enough for one bottom crust.

WELCOME BACK FROM VACATION!

We all seem to go our separate ways during vacations and it is important to catch up when we get back home again. What better way than a cooking spree where everyone gets into the act? Anyone can stir-fry and you might mention to your weight-conscious friends that it is a very lo-cal way to go and still eat well. A Chinese diet is noticeably low in fat and they do cook their vegetables in the healthiest way.

A Stir Fry
Barley Pilaf
Fortune Cookies with Sherbet

A STIR-FRY

protein: 6 g   calories: 250

2 tbsp (30 ml) sesame seeds
4 tbsp (60 ml) vegetable oil
1 onion, cut in thin rings
¼ head of cabbage, shredded
1 zucchini or yellow squash, cut in thin rings
4 carrots, cut in thin rings
¼ lb. (113.4 g) green beans, thinly sliced
1 10-oz. (283.5 g) package frozen snow pea pods
1 tbsp (15 ml) soy sauce
1 tbsp (15 ml) water

1. Set a Chinese wok over medium-high heat. Put in sesame seeds and stir until toasted. Remove.
2. Add 2 tbsp (30 ml) oil and add onion rings. Stir-fry for 2 minutes. Remove.
3. Add cabbage and fry for 4 minutes, tossing constantly. Remove.
4. Stir-fry squash for 1½ minutes. Remove.
5. Add remaining oil to pan and stir-fry carrots for 3 minutes. Remove and add green beans and pea pods. Stir-fry for 2 minutes.
6. Add soy sauce and water and return all vegetables to wok. Stir and toss over medium heat for 1 minute. Sprinkle with sesame seeds and serve immediately.

Yield: 4 servings

BARLEY PILAF

protein: 8 g   calories: 340

2 tbsp (30 ml) butter
2 tbsp (30 ml) oil
1 medium-sized onion, chopped
1 cup (240 ml) medium pearl barley
2 cups (480 ml) vegetable broth
½ cup (120 ml) cottage cheese
½ cup (120 ml) plain yogurt
Salt to taste
Freshly ground pepper
2 tbsp (30 ml) chopped parsley

1. Heat butter and oil in skillet and sauté onion until soft. Add barley to skillet and sauté, stirring, until it looks dull in color.
2. Pour in vegetable broth, reduce heat, cover pan, and cook for about 30 minutes until barley is barely tender.
3. Turn into baking dish and stir in cottage cheese and yogurt. Season to taste with salt and pepper.
4. Cover dish and bake for 1 hour in a preheated 350°F (175°C) oven.
5. Sprinkle with parsley before serving.

Yield: 4 servings

FORTUNE COOKIES

protein: 1 g   calories: 35

> 2 eggs
> ½ cup (120 ml) sugar
> 1 tbsp (15 ml) cold water
> 1 tsp (5 ml) almond extract
> ⅔ cup (160 ml) unbleached white flour

1.   Beat eggs and sugar together until thick and lemon-colored. This will take about 10 minutes with an electric beater. Beat in water, almond extract, and flour.

2.   On well-greased cookie sheets drop spoonfuls of batter to form circles about 2 inches (5 cm) in diameter, 2 inches (5 cm) apart.

3.   Bake in a preheated 350°F (175°C) oven for 12 minutes or until edges are light brown. Remove cookies from sheet one at a time, leaving remainder in oven.

4.   Make up your own fortunes and write on small strips of paper. Put paper fortune on cookie and with fingers fold up and bend into proper shape. Cool.

Yield: about 2 dozen

Note: These become brittle once exposed to air, so work quickly.

A FRENCH CLASS PICNIC

When spring term comes, here's a zingy picnic menu for your French class. After all, who appreciates good food more than the French? Just to keep it well-rounded from a nutrition angle, we've taken the crust from the quiche and put it under the tarts and marinated the zucchini in oil. Did you know that a small amount of vegetable oil is necessary to provide the essential fatty acids in your body?

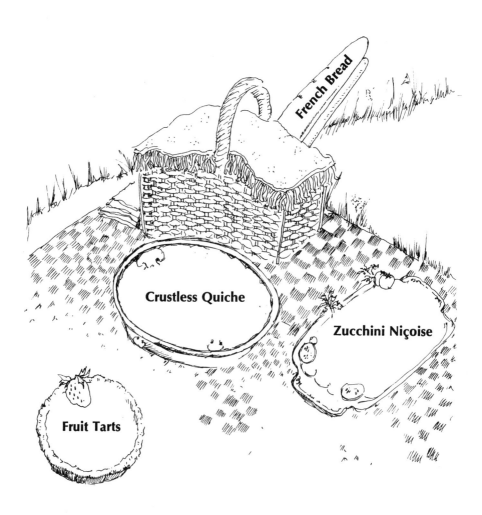

CRUSTLESS QUICHE

protein: 17 g   calories: 275

> 2 tbsp (30 ml) butter or margarine
> ½ lb. (226.80 g) mushrooms, sliced
> 2 cups (480 ml) shredded Swiss or Gruyère cheese
>   (unprocessed)
> 3 eggs
> 2 cups (480 ml) milk
> Salt to taste
> Freshly ground pepper
> ½ tsp (2.5 ml) nutmeg
> ¼ tsp (1.2 ml) dry mustard

1. Heat butter in skillet and sauté mushrooms for 10 minutes.
2. Grease a 9-inch (22.5-cm) pie plate or shallow dish and place mushrooms in bottom. Cover mushrooms with cheese.
3. In bowl, beat together the eggs, milk, and seasonings. Pour into pie plate and place plate on baking sheet to catch any drips.
4. Place in a preheated 350°F (175°C) oven and bake for 30 to 35 minutes until no longer soft in center. Remove from oven and let stand 10 minutes before serving.

Yield: 6 servings

Note: For a picnic, wrap quiche in foil and let stand at room temperature.

ZUCCHINI NIÇOISE

protein: 2 g   calories: 230

6 medium-sized zucchini
Oil for frying
2 tbsp (30 ml) vinegar
6 tbsp (90 ml) oil
1 garlic clove, mashed
2 tbsp (30 ml) fresh dill or 1 tsp (5 ml) dried dill
Salt to taste
Freshly ground pepper
Fresh salad greens
3 tbsp (45 ml) minced parsley
8 cherry tomatoes, halved
8 pitted black olives
1 tsp (5 ml) capers, drained

1.   Cut unpeeled zucchini into ¾-inch (1.9-cm) slices.
2.   Heat about ¼ inch (.6 cm) of oil in skillet over high heat. When oil is smoking, turn heat to medium and put in zucchini slices. Fry a few at a time, about 2 minutes on each side, until golden but still crisp. Drain on paper towels.
3.   Mix together the vinegar, oil, dill, and salt, and pepper. Put fried zucchini slices on salad greens on a large platter. Sprinkle with parsley and garnish with tomatoes and olives. Pour dressing over all.

Yield: 6 servings

Note: To mash garlic easily, place clove on flat surface and hit hard with the handle of a knife or a flat side of a large knife or cleaver. The skin will peel off and the clove will be smashed.

FRUIT TARTS

protein: 5 g   calories: 420

    6 individual pastry tart shells, baked
    1 8-oz. (226.8 g) package cream cheese, softened
    3 tbsp (45 ml) orange juice concentrate (frozen)
    Fresh blueberries, peaches, or strawberries
    ½ cup (120 ml) crab apple or currant jelly
    2 tbsp (30 ml) water

1.   Beat cream cheese with orange juice concentrate until smooth. Spread in bottom of baked tart shells. Cover with fresh fruit.

2.   Heat together the jelly and water until liquid. Brush or spoon over fruit and cream cheese, covering the top completely.

3.   Refrigerate tarts until ready to serve.

Yield: 6 servings

TAKE A BIKE HIKE

We're stuffing everything into a saddlebag or knapsack for the bike hike and it seems easier to stuff everything ahead of time. Eggs, celery, cucumbers, dates—look around and see what additional foods you can think of that can be filled with other foods. You need energy for those hills, so pack some of our snack packs to munch on as you pedal along and put the milk shake into a lightweight plastic Thermos. Biking is one of the best all-around exercises going and if you can include some swimming, you can double your lunch and not worry an ounce.

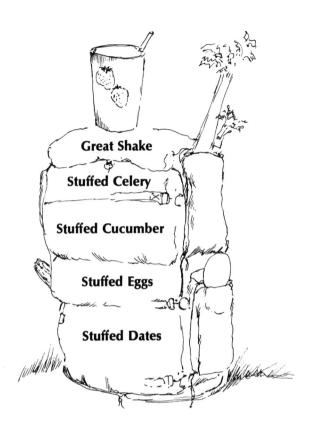

Great Shake

Stuffed Celery

Stuffed Cucumber

Stuffed Eggs

Stuffed Dates

KNAPSACK STUFFED LUNCH

2 celery stalks stuffed with peanut butter
protein: 9 g   calories: 200

2 eggs deviled with curry powder and 1 tbsp (15 ml) mayonnaise
protein: 11 g   calories: 250

1 medium cucumber stuffed with 3-oz. (85.5 g) package chive
   cream cheese
protein: 9 g   calories: 350

6 dates stuffed with whole blanched almonds
protein: 2 g   calories: 170

GREAT SHAKE

protein: 24 g   calories: 315

½ 10-oz. (141.8 g) package frozen strawberries
1 cup (240 ml) dry skim milk powder
2 cups (480 ml) cold water
1 tsp (5 ml) vanilla
½ tsp (2.5 ml) almond extract
1 tbsp (15 ml) honey

1. Put all ingredients into blender and blend until smooth.

Yield: 2 servings

APPENDIX: CALORIE AND PROTEIN TABLES

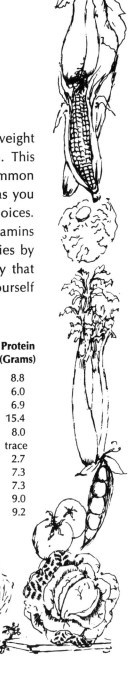

CHOOSING YOUR CALORIES

You should choose calories selectively—to control weight *and* ensure yourself the proper nutrients for good health. This chart gives average protein values and calories in common foods. Protein is just one nutrient, but when you watch it as you choose calories, you are apt to think more about all food choices. Give yourself the benefit of foods high in minerals and vitamins before adding additional calorie foods. Be guided in calories by your own needs. You are an individual and it is your body that you are taking care of. In this respect, it pays to think of yourself first.

DAIRY FOODS	Size of Portion	Calories	Protein (Grams)
Buttermilk	1 cup (8 oz., 244 g)	88	8.8
Cheese, American	slice (1 oz., 28 g)	104	6.0
Cheese, Cheddar	slice (1 oz., 28 g)	113	6.9
Cheese, cottage	½ cup (4 oz., 113 g)	120	15.4
Cheese, Swiss	slice (1 oz., 28 g)	103	8.0
Cream, sour	1 tbsp (12 g)	25	trace
Ice cream, vanilla	½ cup (¼ pt., 66 g)	138	2.7
Milk, whole	1 cup (8 oz., 244 g)	150	7.3
Milk, lowfat	1 cup (8 oz., 244 g)	118	7.3
Yogurt, plain	1 cup (8 oz., 244 g)	150	9.0
Yogurt, strawberry	1 cup (8 oz., 244 g)	225	9.2

EGGS AND LEGUMES	Size of Portion	Calories	Protein (Grams)
Egg, fried	large (50 g)	108	6.9
Egg, hard-cooked	large (50 g)	82	6.5
Egg, scrambled	large (64 g)	111	7.2
Peanut butter	2 tbsp (32 g) smooth	186	8.9
Peanuts, salted	¼ cup (36 g)	211	9.4

FRUITS

	Size of Portion	Calories	Protein (Grams)
Apple	medium (138 g)	80	0.3
Applesauce	½ cup (128 g) sweetened, canned	116	0.3
Apricots, dried	4 halves (4 g)	39	0.8
Banana	medium (119 g)	101	1.3
Cantaloupe	¼ medium (120 g)	29	0.7
Grapefruit	½ medium (118 g)	48	0.6
Grapes	½ cup (71 g)	48	0.4
Orange juice	½ cup (4 oz., 125 g) frozen, reconstituted	56	0.9
Orange	medium (131 g)	65	1.3
Peaches	½ cup (50 g) sliced, canned in heavy syrup	39	0.2
Pear	medium (166 g)	101	1.2
Raisins	4½ tbsp (1½ oz., 43 g)	123	1.1
Strawberries	½ cup (75 g)	28	0.5

VEGETABLES AND SALADS

	Size of Portion	Calories	Protein (Grams)
Asparagus	4 spears, ½ cup (60 g)	12	1.3
Beans, green	½ cup (63 g) cooked	16	1.0
Beets	½ cup (83 g) sliced	31	0.8
Broccoli, stalk	½ cup (78 g)	20	2.4
Carrots	½ cup (73 g)	22	0.7
Celery sticks	raw, 8-inch (20-cm) stalk (2 oz., 57 g)	10	0.5
Coleslaw	½ cup (57 g) with mayonnaise dressing	82	0.7
Corn	½ cup (83 g)	114	2.2
Greens	½ cup (78 g) cooked	17	1.9
Lettuce	1/6 medium head, raw ½ cup (76 g)	10	0.7
Onions	½ cup (105 g)	30	1.3
Peas, green	½ cup (80 g)	54	4.1
Potato, baked	large (5 oz., 142 g)	132	3.7
Potato, boiled	2 small (4.3 oz., 122 g)	79	2.3
Squash, summer	½ cup (105 g) yellow	16	1.1
Tossed salad	¾ cup (59 g) lettuce, carrot, green pepper, radish	13	0.7
Zucchini	½ cup (105 g)	15	0

BREADS AND CEREALS

	Size of Portion	Calories	Protein (Grams)
Bread, white	slice (4/5 oz., 23 g)	61	2.0
Bread, whole wheat	slice (4/5 oz., 23 g)	55	2.4
Cornbread	2½-by-3 inch (6.25-by-7.5 cm) (85 g)	191	6.0
Corn flakes	¾ cup (19 g)	72	1.5
Crackers, graham	2-by-2½-inch (5-by-6.25 cm) square (14 g)	54	1.1
Noodles, egg	½ cup (80 g) cooked	100	3.3
Oatmeal	½ cup (120 g) cooked	66	2.4
Rice	½ cup (103 g) cooked	112	2.1
Tortilla, corn	6-inch (15-cm) diameter (30 g)	63	1.5

DESSERTS

Cake, sponge	1/12 of 10-inch (25-cm) cake (66 g)	196	5.0
Custard	½ cup (133 g)	152	7.2
Doughnut	32 g	125	1.5
Pie, apple	1/6 of 9-inch (22.5-cm) pie (158 g)	403	3.5
Popcorn	1 cup (6 g) plain	23	0.8

MISCELLANEOUS

Butter	1 tsp (5 g)	36	trace
French dressing	1 tbsp (16 g)	66	0.1
Jelly	1 tbsp (18 g)	49	0
Mayonnaise	1 tbsp (14 g)	101	0.2
Sugar	1 tsp (4 g)	14	0

FOR
FURTHER READING

Arnold, Pauline, and White, Percival. *Food Facts for Young People*. New York: Holiday House, Inc., 1968.

Harris, F. L. and Withers, R. T. *Your Foods Book*. Boston: D. C. Heath and Co., 1964.

Lappe, Frances, and Ewald, Ellen. *Great Meatless Meals*. New York: Ballantine Books, 1974.

Robertson, Laurel, Flinders, Carol, and Godfrey, Bronwen. *Laurel's Kitchen*. Berkeley, Calif.: Nilgiri Press, 1976.

Salmon, Margaret. *Food Facts for Teenagers*. Springfield, Ill.: Charles C. Thomas, 1965.

Stare, Frederick J., M.D. *Eating for Good Health*. Garden City, N.Y.: Doubleday and Co., 1964.

INDEX